D1530812

PRAISE FOR RICHARD RYBOLT'S

75 WAYS TO BEAT DEPRESSION

"Rybolt's *75 Ways to Beat Depression* is a much needed pick-me-up for the community of depression—for those suffering from depression, as well as their therapists, family, and associates. His strategies for offsetting depression's effects are from his experience, with sound rationale, and easy to understand and implement. A must for everyone's resource shelf—I'll certainly keep it on mine!"

—PIERCE J. HOWARD, PhD,
author of *The Owner's Manual for the Brain,*
Director of Research, Center for Applied Cognitive Studies,
Charlotte, NC

"Richard Rybolt offers a creative new approach to beating depression and dealing with the demoralizing effects that accompany this illness. *75 Ways to Beat Depression* is a small book in volume but it provides a wealth of valuable information and self-help tools in an easy-to-read journalistic style. After successfully learning to recognize, self-monitor, and free himself from his own 'battle of the blues,' Rybolt gives hope and help to others by illustrating through personal experience how it is possible to overcome depression and return to a happy, productive life. Mr. Rybolt demonstrates the importance of getting to the root of the problem, the very prerequisite for a new appreciation of life—a life free of fear, anxiety, and shame."

—NANCY ROSENFELD,
coauthor of *New Hope for People with Bipolar Disorder*

"Richard Rybolt's unique book—part memoir, part inspiration, and part self-help—is like a trusted companion that guides those besieged with depression in their journey towards a life abundant with love, meaning, and even joy. Rybolt's recount of his recovery is of special significance to men, who often need reassurance that seeking help and reaching out to others is not a sign of weakness, but an act of courage and a hallmark of inner strength."

—RANDI KREGER,
coauthor of *Stop Walking on Eggshells*

A
successful horticulturist
and property developer for much of
his life, **RICHARD RYBOLT** is now an
active crusader for overcoming depression and
a strong ally of the despondent. He has helped
establish support groups, education seminars, and
healing networks, and has personally coached and
befriended those suffering from plights similar to his
own. He has told his story of recovery and
inspiration on various radio and television shows
and before live audiences. The author of *No
Chairs Make for Short Meetings*, he lives
with his wife on a small farm in
upstate New York.

75
WAYS TO
BEAT
DEPRESSION

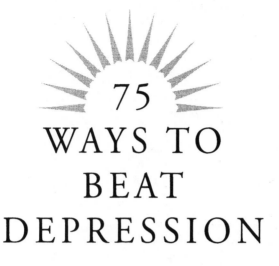

75
WAYS TO
BEAT
DEPRESSION

*WORDS OF HOPE
& SOLUTIONS THAT WORK*

RICHARD RYBOLT

MARLOWE & COMPANY
NEW YORK

75 WAYS TO BEAT DEPRESSION: *Words of Hope and Solutions that Work*
Copyright © 2005 by Richard Rybolt

Published by
Marlowe & Company
An Imprint of Avalon Publishing Group Incorporated
245 West 17th Street • 11th Floor
New York, NY 10011-5300

AVALON
Publishing group Incorporated

All rights reserved. No part of this book may be reproduced in whole
or in part without written permission from the publisher, except by reviewers
who may quote brief excerpts in connection with a review in a newspaper,
magazine, or electronic publication; nor may any part of this book be
reproduced, stored in a retrieval system, or transmitted in any form
or by any means electronic, mechanical, photocopying, recording,
or other, without written permission from the publisher.

Library of Congress Cataloging-in-Publication Data
Rybolt, Richard, 1937–
75 ways to beat depression : words of hope and solutions that work /
Richard Rybolt.—Seventy-five ways to beat depression
p. cm.
ISBN 1-56924-357-3 (pbk.)
1. Depression, Mental—Popular works. I. Title.
RC537.R97 2006
616.85'2706—dc22
2005012742

ISBN-13: 978-1-56924-357-2

Designed by Pauline Neuwirth, Neuwirth & Associates, Inc.

Printed in the United States of America

Dedicated to My Sister

Dear Martha,

You were my second mother, the one who cared for me and our brothers during the lean times of childhood, when both Mom and Daddy worked long hours to make ends meet. I still wonder where we might have ended up if you had not been there to bandage our skinned knees, patch our broken hearts, and referee our childish spats. Although you were little more than a child yourself, you guided us down that narrow road of virtue with the tough but tender love of a mother.

It was your own courageous fight with depression that inspired me to write this book, and I wish that I could hand you the first copy. But Heaven is beyond my reach, so I offer it in your memory, to the countless others who are detoured on this rough and lonely road called depression. My prayer is that this book may help to illuminate their pathway and provide positive proof that good can come even from the darkest places . . . proof that faith and love can keep us going until we reach a bright and better day.

Thank you, big sister, for your lessons of courage. Tonight I will look for you among the brightest stars that grace the heavens of eternity.

Until we meet again,
Dick

The information in this book is intended to help readers make informed decisions about their health and the health of their loved ones. It is not intended to be a substitute for treatment by or the advice and care of a professional health care provider. While the author and publisher have endeavored to ensure that the information presented is accurate and up-to-date, they are not responsible for adverse effects or consequences sustained by any person using this book.

CONTENTS

INTRODUCTION

There were mornings when depression pinned me to the bed with a fist in the pit of my stomach that twisted like a knot... mornings when my mind begged me not to get up and face the world again. There were days when I felt like the sky was caving in as I tried to hold it up. Frequently, I couldn't concentrate enough to read a newspaper.

I remember countless nights when depression awakened me long before dawn. I would lie in the darkness, tossing and turning, unable to banish the voices of impending doom from my head. Finally, I would drag myself out of bed and out to the recliner on the back porch to wait for the first signs of morning light. Ever so slowly, the sun would crawl over the treetops to shrink depression's shadows and deliver the slim hope of getting through another day.

Growing up poor on our little farm in Ohio, I learned early to be a worker—and a fighter. Our family worked hard for what little we had, and between the weather, bill collectors, and my alcoholic father, we seemed to be in a constant battle to keep it.

Somehow, from those humble beginnings, I rose to the ranks of prosperous millionaire businessman. With wealth, my confidence grew. I believed that nothing could come between me and success, much less between me and happiness.

Then came depression. I knew right away that something was dreadfully wrong, but I had no idea what. Fatigue and anger paralyzed me; I went through the motions of living with an apathetic numbness hidden in my heart. It sounds like a cliché, but the colors of my life faded until nothing remained but drab shades of gray. I told myself that I was tired and "stressed out." I tried taking time off, tried doing nothing. It only deepened my melancholy. Soon I began to imagine that I had every possible illness, all the while denying the diagnosis of my family doctor—depression. Depression was a dreaded word that described people who were mentally weak, people who let themselves be sad. It certainly couldn't apply to a person like me. Finally, when no other diagnosis would fit, I reluctantly admitted that *maybe* my problem *was* depression, but even then I was sure it would last only a short time and I'd be back to normal again.

Months became years as this illness chased me deep into the valleys of despair, harassing me for reasons I'll probably never understand. Why me? Why me? Why me? It's the depression sufferer's most common refrain. I wasted hours navel-gazing, searching all the way back to my early childhood, determined to find someone or something to blame. I'd always been a person of great optimism, but now I had to practically *will* myself to accomplish anything. Eventually I came to understand that why and where my depression came from didn't matter a whit. Whatever the reason, depression had twisted itself tightly around me and I could either let it choke the joy out of my life or find a way to stop it.

Being a businessman had taught me how to solve problems, but it didn't prepare me for this battle. After many frustrating tries, I acknowledged that depression was the toughest challenge I'd faced in a lifetime of struggles. The word *hell* can't begin to describe how shattering depression was for me. Perhaps because my youth was grounded in adversity, I kept fighting . . . kept praying . . . kept searching for some way out of this wretched ordeal. In time, a new and stronger person emerged from somewhere deep inside of me, a person less arrogant, less complacent than before. I no longer sought perfection for myself or the world. I began to find unspeakable joy in the everyday adventures of living. The brambles of life remained, but the berries tasted so much sweeter than before.

Depression is always a family affair, and it was my wife Anita who guided our family through the darkness of my depressive years. Her encouraging notes to me, which she frequently left between the pages of my journal, provided the lift to keep me searching for solutions to my ordeal. I've shared several of Anita's notes with readers of this book, to illustrate the vital role of family and friends in helping a loved one recover from depression.

The ideas and tactics I used to drive away depression are all contained in this small book. *75 Ways to Beat Depression* is designed to offer hope and help to others who are looking for pathways to move out of the shadows and back toward sunshine again. I'm not a doctor or a therapist. I can offer no guarantees for recovery. What I can promise is that everything in this book comes from the trenches of my own war with despair.

This book is designed so you can easily flip through the pages and find the help that is relevant to your needs. Some of the solutions will become mainstays that you will use often to help restore clear thinking. Other ideas can be skipped completely because they won't feel right for you. I would, however, urge you to try each solution at least once or twice, even though it may seem too basic or even downright silly. Simple therapies often have significant potential to improve your moods.

My greatest hope is that by applying these ideas, you and yours may also be lifted to the higher ground of hope and recovery.

WAYS TO
BEAT
DEPRESSION

SEEK HELP

— FROM MY JOURNAL —

I will never forget the day my family doctor first talked to me about depression and recommended I see a psychiatrist. I sat there stupefied, staring at the floor. "Psychiatrist? No way," I thought.

Well, that was months ago, and I've finally agreed to go. Today was my appointment and I didn't have the foggiest notion about what to expect from this doctor named Leighton. Fear and anxiety nearly had me in a state of hysteria by the time I got there.

I had hardly sat down before the doctor came into the waiting room, introduced himself, and motioned me down the hall. I was relieved to find that, other than his bright purple shirt, he looked pretty much like anyone else. Surveying the room, I found it a rather typical doctor's office except it was larger, the chairs were plusher and the floor was covered with thick carpet. Dr. Leighton waved his hand toward a chair, and after a bit of chitchat, he began asking more serious questions. As the conversation continued, I found myself doing most of the talking, and before long I could tell that Dr.

Leighton was about to conclude. I still had that one haunting question in my mind that had plagued me for weeks.

"Doctor Leighton," I began, "what do you see as the prognosis for my problem?" I purposely avoided the words depression *and mental illness.*

He assured me that with medication and counseling, I could expect improvement soon.

The visit over, I returned to the car, got in, and pulled the door shut. The relief was so overwhelming that I burst into tears, sobbing uncontrollably. I was not going crazy. Dr. Leighton had given me my first real hope that I would be all right.

THINGS TO CONSIDER

The first time your doctor used the word *depression*, you probably felt like a truck had run over you. The doctor probably went on to clarify and explain, but the chances are you heard little of what he or she said because a much louder voice—fear—had entered your mind. Maybe the words *counseling, therapist* or *psychiatrist* floated out to reach your consciousness, but you prayed the doctor wasn't referring to you. Half of your fearful thinking was focused on denial—"I can't have depression"—and the other half visualized a dark, uncertain future. It's likely that you already suspected depression, so the diagnosis should have come as no surprise, but even this didn't soften the blow. You were stunned. Shattered! You had been pushed across that wretched line of admitting your depression and you had no idea how to get back.

The good news is that such a reckoning marks the point at which recovery can begin. Some people can cross quickly over the line separating denial from acceptance; for others it may take months or even years. Denying depression as your problem traps you with little possibility of correcting it. Accepting this diagnosis doesn't imply that you are weak or at fault. It simply means that you now know who your enemy is.

TRY THIS . . .

> The place to begin your battle with this illness is by accepting depression as the source of your mood problems. Make a pledge to yourself to do whatever it takes to find the best people, therapies, and resources for recovery.

2

SOLUTION

KNOW YOUR OPPONENT

— FROM MY JOURNAL —

Today I feel like I'm wearing shoes filled with concrete. My feet are so heavy that it takes a conscious effort just to lift them. Dragging myself around like this makes it tough to accomplish anything. Fatigue was among the earliest symptoms of this illness, but at the beginning I had no idea that depression was the cause. So I blamed it on my blood-pressure medicine. . . . Blamed it on job stress. . . . Blamed it on Chronic Fatigue Syndrome.

I remember how my doctor referred me to several medical specialists who found no physical problem, yet my symptoms continued. I remember how I hated seeing the light of morning come creeping into my bedroom, knowing I had hardly slept at all. Depression's uncertainty is difficult to deal with, especially when it makes you doubt yourself.

I remember getting lost as a small child in a J.C. Penney's department store and the terrorizing fear I felt when I could not find my mother and siblings. The fact that people were all around me did nothing to relieve my sense of being utterly alone. This is reminiscent of my feelings of isolation when depression settles in.

I wish now I had acted on my doctor's advice to see a psychiatrist when she first suggested the possibility of depression, but I flatly refused (lying that I was feeling better). I stalled for months more before I reluctantly made that first visit to the psychiatrist and heard that dreaded diagnosis, depression. Just hearing that word struck me with a deep sense of doom that made me feel like my life was over. I'm beginning to see now that it wasn't the end of my life but the beginning of my recovery. Melancholy still slips in and out of my life, but I'm more hopeful now that I have some idea who the enemy is, and I can sense that I'm moving in the direction of recovery.

THINGS TO CONSIDER

Too often, depression makes you feel like you're boxing in the dark with an invisible opponent. However, the sooner you accept the fact that depression is your problem, the sooner you can begin your journey back. Fatigue, headaches, stomach pains, insomnia, poor appetite, and memory loss are only a few of the many confusing symptoms that depression shares with other illnesses. With the help of your doctor, you can begin sorting out these symptoms and placing the blame where it belongs. Once you understand the symptoms associated with your depression, you can stop wasting time trying to place blame elsewhere.

Understanding more about this illness allows you to better tolerate the difficulties it provides. Accurate information is an important tool in your battle with depression, and there are many resources to provide it. These include mental health organizations, excellent books, web sites, and qualified health care professionals. You may also find solutions and comfort by sharing your concerns with others who have personally experienced this illness. Good information about depression will help you map a better route for your own recovery.

TRY THIS . . .

Make a list of specific sources that you plan to pursue in your effort to learn more about depression and the solutions that may work best for you.

NOTE: Pages 237 through 240 of this book provide a list of organizations and internet sites that offer resources to help solve your mood problems.

3
SOLUTION

SING YOUR OWN PRAISES

— FROM MY JOURNAL —

Depression torments me in many ways, but none as abhorrent as those voices of doom that so often occupy my mind. It often seems as if someone has planted a miniature device in my head that plays only negative recordings. These voices threaten and ridicule me with their repulsive insults and accusations. Their clear implication is always the same: that I'm mentally weak and that disaster lies ahead.

Last week I was certain that everyone in my office was whispering lies about me behind my back. When the stock market plunged recently, I worried that I had fallen into financial jeopardy. And when Anita was late getting home from shopping today, the word "accident" filled my mind with panic. In fact, these voices often trick me into attacking myself with words like You can't do anything right, or You screwed up again. I should be smart enough not to beat up on myself, but depression fools me into doing it anyway.

I'm constantly searching for the "off" switches to shut down those menacing mind voices. I've found that when I pull myself away from the TV and get out to the garage to work on the antique cabinet I'm refinishing, that helps to clear my mind and restore my perspective. Playing "fetch" with our puppy helps. Exercise, music, reading, and dozens of other enjoyable diversions all tend to stop those negative tapes from playing in my mind, but still they come back. I've got to find some way to stop these wretched lies for good.

Things to Consider

Almost everyone struggling with depression knows about the internal voices of doom that fill your mind with lies: vicious lies that your family doesn't love you anymore, that your friends are whispering about you behind your back, that your job is in jeopardy; insidious lies that slowly penetrate your psyche with their threats of impending disaster, that predict a future so bleak that retreat often seems your only option.

Interrupting these menacing voices and redirecting your mind toward positive thinking is essential for conquering depression. One effective way to accomplish this is to literally make your own recording. Use a disk or a tape to list all your positive attributes. Describe your talents, abilities, and accomplishments. Expound on family, friends, and associates who believe in you. If you prefer, you can pretend the recording is introducing you as special guest at an important banquet, or you may think of it as an expanded version of your employment resume. Be sure to include a pledge to yourself that no matter what happens, you *will* find a way to triumph over depression.

TRY THIS . . .

Make your own recording based on the ideas offered above. Say whatever you like, but don't be bashful about singing your own praises. Play this recording when you're driving, exercising, house-cleaning, etc. Play it often. If you get tired of hearing it, make a new one. If you accept the silliness of it, it's fun, and it can bolster your self-esteem more than you might imagine. (If you're reluctant or unable to tape the message, write it.)

4

HELP OTHERS—HELP YOURSELF

— FROM MY JOURNAL —

*A*few months back, I got suckered into helping my neighbor Rocky, simply because I couldn't think of an excuse that seemed plausible enough to refuse. I was raking the lawn when he started telling me the story of his recently diagnosed Hodgkin's disease, and I felt cornered into listening. He eventually worked his way around to the difficulty of getting to his radiation treatments, then asked if I'd consider driving him to the hospital on occasion.

If my foot could have reached my rear end, I'd have given myself a swift kick for not having the guts to simply say "no." After all, my depression was making it tough to just drag myself out of bed in the morning. Surely, I wasn't the right guy to be helping someone else.

Nevertheless, the following Tuesday I found myself driving Rocky to his radiation treatment. He was talking about his concern for his family and the fear of losing his job. "Don't get mixed up in this," I kept telling myself. But somewhere in the discussion, I forgot about my own concerns and became involved in his. In the weeks since, I've driven Rocky to his radiation treatment many times and helped out wherever I could, but mostly we just talked— about him, about me, about life.

Today is Rocky's first day back to work. The radiation treatments are over and his prognosis is greatly improved. When we had coffee before he left this morning, he acted like a kid on his first day of school.

Thinking back on this whole episode, I'm beginning to understand the huge psychological boost that I received by helping him. All along I thought that I was the giver. This wonderful turn of events reminds me of the boomerang that I'd throw as a kid. I loved to watch it circle wide, then come right back to me—just like the gift of giving.

Constantly focusing on yourself is one of the problems that feed depressive illness. It causes you to worry about almost everything. Are you getting old? Are you getting fat? Are you losing your mind? You fret about your work, your car, even your cat. Apprehension like this can burden you with so many negatives that hope finds no place to grow.

One way to reduce this destructive self-absorption is to find someone else to be the focus of your concern. Perhaps you know an elderly neighbor who needs help with house or yard chores. Maybe you could befriend a coworker with an ill child, or help out at the local animal shelter. There are lots of places your help would be appreciated, and assisting someone else boosts your self-esteem and increases your sense of well-being. You might have thought that helping other people with their problems would increase your own depression, but that's rarely the way it works out. Depression usually diminishes as you follow the pathway of service to others.

TRY THIS . . .

Make a list of friends who might need a hand, but also investigate volunteer opportunities. When you find the situation that feels right, sign on for a trial period before making a substantial commitment.

CONNECT WITH THE DIVINE

— FROM MY JOURNAL —

This afternoon I began to feel like my office walls were closing in around me. My shouting match with our maintenance manager over labor costs disturbed me. I couldn't keep pretending that everything was just fine—I was ready to explode! Was there a friend I could talk with, someplace to collect myself where people would not think I was just whining again?

I left the office and drove around aimlessly. I could think of no place to go. Then I remembered the little-used chapel at our church. I pulled up on the side street and I found the rear door open, so I was able to slip in unnoticed. I've always loved the place; it reminds me of a hidden room in a castle, with its old stone walls and heavy dark beams. I sat in utter silence except for the creaking of the wood pew I rested on.

At first I felt I had no right to be there. I've been called a lot of things over the years but "religious" has never been one of them. Yet the peace and solitude felt so good to me that I held my face in my hands and tried to ease the pain throbbing in my head. I tried to pray but tears, not words, came out instead. "God—help me, God," was all I could whisper. Slowly, after what seemed like hours, a new sense of serenity erased the anger and anxiety of my mind.

Leaving the chapel, I felt renewed. My racing mind had quieted. God had answered the prayers I could not pray by giving me a new measure of hope. I could face the world again.

THINGS TO CONSIDER

Faith may not provide an all-encompassing solution for depression, but for many people it has the potential to expand life's perspective so that depression appears not as a dead end but as a temporary detour on life's long road.

Many people who struggle with this illness are able to develop or maintain a strong relationship with the Almighty, and there's substantial evidence that this can help restore mental health. It's often said that "faith can move mountains," and one of those mountains may be your depression.

Others find that the trials of depression have pushed God away, and some people even believe God is the villain who singled them out to suffer this illness. Although each of us must assemble our own puzzle regarding faith, there are innumerable resources to help us sort through the many pieces. Devout friends, clergy, books, tapes, and places of worship are but a few of the opportunities available for enriching your faith.

Prayer is one technique worth trying. Though it's different for each of us, prayer may comfort even nonbelievers in times of crisis and adversity. Prayer works—if you *believe* it works.

TRY THIS . . .

The lesson of this exercise is that prayer can take place at any time and anywhere you choose. No place is off-limits. Name three of the most unusual places where you've ever prayed, and resolve to give it a try next time you're in need.

6
SOLUTION

CONFRONT PANIC ATTACKS

— From My Journal —

I had a harrowing drive to the village of Medina today! It usually takes me forty-five minutes to get there, so I decided to save a little time and take the nine-mile shortcut through the state wildlife preserve. Everything was fine until I turned off the main highway onto that isolated stretch of road with no houses on it. Shortly after I made that turn, a sense of impending doom grabbed my throat, and the farther I went, the worse it got, until I could hardly breathe. My heart was racing so loudly that it sounded like a drum ready to explode. I felt like I was abandoned in the middle of nowhere.

"Turn back! Turn back!" was the message that flashed in my mind. I can only credit my stubbornness for making me grip the wheel even tighter as I kept going. At one point, I pulled out my wallet and flipped it open to a photo of Anita and the kids. I'm not sure why I did this except that I felt so isolated—so alone.

After what seemed like an eternity, I finally reached the busy highway again and my panic dissipated almost as quickly as it had come. What embarrasses me as I write this journal note is that I knew, even then, there was absolutely nothing to fear. Still, I couldn't stop this menacing terror from seizing my mind. I've experienced panic attacks before and, every time their horror shocks me anew.

Today I didn't turn back; I kept on going in spite of everything. Someone who has never experienced a panic attack might think this a pretty small accomplishment. To me it felt like breaking through another prison wall. I'd like to believe that my panic attacks are over, but I doubt that. I am willing to bet, however, that no road will ever traumatize me quite like that again.

Things to Consider

A terrifying three-minute panic attack can feel like an eternity. While the basis of such attacks is *irrational* fear, the terror they cause is as real as any you'll ever face. You may think you're going crazy, having a heart attack, or worse. Controlling these attacks begins with an understanding of their nature and your ability to arm yourself with the truth.

Although panic attacks are very frightening, they rarely involve any serious medical repercussions. Even though your pounding heart feels like it is about to jump out of your chest, it won't. Simply knowing that fear and panic attacks are common to depression helps to take away the surprise element that can lead to hysteria.

There are various coping mechanisms that can reduce your feelings of helplessness when you face these assaults. Some people can reverse an attack simply by yelling *Stop!* This tends to grab your mind for the few seconds needed to bring you back to reality. Other distractions people use are starting a conversation with someone next to them, making a cup of tea, or fiddling with the television remote. Anything that switches your focus, for even a few seconds, can allow this wave of irrational fear to pass as your mind grasps the truth: *You are just fine.* Every time you confront these fears with a positive response, you reduce the power they hold over you.

TRY THIS . . .

Make a list of three simple actions that you would consider trying to reduce the impact of a panic attack. A good way to begin your list is by thinking of things that you can do almost anywhere to quickly distract your panic thoughts. For example: Start a conversation with someone near you.

NOTE: If you're plagued by panic attacks, seek professional help. But remind yourself that panic attacks rarely cause serious medical problems.

7
SOLUTION

LEAN ON ME

— FROM MY JOURNAL —

I FOUND THIS NOTE STICKING OUT OF MY JOURNAL THIS MORNING.
ANITA MUST HAVE PUT IT THERE LAST NIGHT AFTER I WENT TO BED.

Dick,

I know these past few weeks have been tough ones. I see you dragging yourself around trying to find the strength and energy to keep going. I just wanted to remind you that I struggle with you— we're in this predicament together for as long as it takes. We will conquer this disorder. Why am I so sure? Because I know your determination and your persistence (probably what I've called "stubbornness" at times!).

I also want you to know that I don't see this ordeal as a weakness of your character but a test of your strength. I'm proud of the way you have faced these difficult times with your "try anything" approach. I have long admired the way you've faced problems in business, diligently searching out every solution to find the right answer. It's evident that you're using that same strategy to fight this battle.

My regret, in all of this, is that I can't somehow shoulder more of the load. We've always worked things out together, so please don't exclude me now. So many times in the past I've leaned on you, could it be your turn to lean a little more on me?

Love,

Anita

Things to Consider

There's a mistake in the wedding vows that most of us take. The words *for better or worse* should really read *for better* and *worse* because life always poses both the good and the bad. Understanding this aspect of living can soften the suffering that comes with your depression.

All of us need to become better at leaning on others in tough times—and willing to return the favor in good times. The problem with depression is that while it smacks you around, it's also whispering in your ear that you are a wimp if you reach out to ask help from others. This is one more of depression's lies that you must recognize in order to expose and treat the illness. Letting your family, friends, and health care professionals help you will speed you along the road to recovery.

Leaning a little doesn't mean that you're weak or that you're giving up; it means that you have the good judgment to use all the available resources to fight life's tough battles. The old saying that two heads are better than one is never more true than when you choose to reach out for help in fighting depression.

TRY THIS . . .

Make a list of areas in which you could use a little more help and think about the right people to assist you. (Chances are good that some of them have already offered their assistance.) Then reach out and accept that help graciously, with the full assurance that you will have many future opportunities to return the favor to others.

TALK TO YOURSELF

— From My Journal —

*A*s I was shaving this morning, I stood back and took a hard look at myself in the mirror. Depression has been reminding me of my shortcomings so often that I was almost afraid to look at the guy staring back at me. Lately, I've begun to imagine myself looking like the forlorn Ringling Brothers circus clown, Emmett Kelly. I remember that as a small boy, visiting the circus for the first time, I saw this immortal clown stop right in front of my seat, staring at me with the most pathetic look I'd ever seen. I still hate to admit it, but he scared me so badly that I cried. And I feel a little like crying today when I think about how depression has so convincingly distorted the person that I really am.

I continued to stand there looking at myself in the mirror for several minutes, finally succumbing to the urge to roll my eyes to the center and twist my face up like I used to do when I was a kid. I was surprised to find that the dimple that the girls used to tease me about was still there. Then I tried curving my lips into a broad smile—it worked. Checking closer, even the mischievous glint in my eyes that used to cause trepidation among my teachers was faintly evident. Next, I surprised myself by saying out loud, "You still look pretty darn good." That's how I got started talking to myself. Perhaps I stretched the truth just a little when I said, "You haven't changed a bit." I gave myself a subtle wink, shut off the light, and pulled the bathroom door shut behind me. It felt great to discover today that my old self was still there beneath the mask of depression.

THINGS TO CONSIDER

Talking to yourself can be an effective method of battling depression. Your own words of confidence and hope, whether whispered or shouted, have surprising power to penetrate your mind and improve your outlook. One useful "self-talk" tactic is to stand in front of a mirror and carry on a two-sided conversation with yourself, as if you were talking to a friend. The amazing thing about self-talk is that your mind will react to your own voice almost as if it belonged to someone else.

There are many uplifting things you could talk about: how you've faced up to this baffling depression opponent by refusing to hide in isolation, your determined effort to search out information and solutions for healing, or how you've fought to pull yourself up after each depressive ordeal instead of indulging in self-pity. Remind yourself that a promising future lies ahead.

Acknowledge that regardless of future difficulties, you're already a survivor. And each day that you survive you become more resilient than before.

TRY THIS . . .

> Look for opportunities to use "self-talk" to eliminate negative feelings and expand positive aspects of your life. Try preparing by completing the following statements:
>
> > I will talk to myself about . . .
> > I will remind myself to . . .
> > I will have a conversation with myself in the mirror and promise myself that . . .

9

SOLUTION

EXAMINE YOUR FEARS

— FROM MY JOURNAL —

I'm actually afraid of being afraid, terrified that my fear will destroy me.

I realize that my fearfulness didn't originate with depression, although this illness has magnified it. Thinking back to childhood, I think I've always been more fearful than my brothers. I remember one occasion when a delivery man rang our door bell and we all trailed after my mother as she went to answer it. Hiding behind her skirt, I refused to accept the lollipop the man offered even though my brothers grabbed theirs without hesitation. Why was I so petrified, even back then?

And I remember the time during my army stint when I was sent to the commissary to pick up some kitchen supplies. On the way back, I got lost on a road that wound through a muddy training field. My Jeep was plastered with mud and I knew I'd be in trouble when I got back. Sure enough, the first sergeant wanted to see me. I rushed over to his office; he was busy. So I waited on a bench outside his door, worried to death that he'd throw me in the clink, or worse.

Almost three hours later, his office door finally opened and he brushed by me with hardly a glance. "Wash that Jeep, soldier, and have it back here within an hour." With those words, he was gone. I had made myself sick with worry—for nothing.

I hate to admit it, but there are so many things I'm afraid of, like cancer, heart attacks, strokes, and almost every other ailment. A minor hiccup of the securities market starts a retirement-related panic response. I know of no valid reason for this fear that runs rampant over my life and blots out the joy and happiness that would otherwise prevail. They say everyone has a dark side to their life, so fear must be mine. I rarely talk about it to anyone, except my journal. I try not to admit it, even to myself.

THINGS TO CONSIDER

Fear can never be divided into the real or imagined. All fear is real and it races across your mind like a news alert on the bottom of your TV—*trouble ahead*—*possible disaster imminent*. While the fear is real, most of the threats are false, especially those originating from depression. Yet fear *can* have value; some warnings need to be heeded. Pains in your chest, a loud clanking in your furnace, or a scraping sound when you apply your car brakes . . . these can create fear that needs to at least be checked out to determine if action is needed.

The solution to combating your fear is to examine every threat and decide whether it's valid. People often fail to do this because they are afraid of fear itself. So they toss all their warnings of fear into a dark closet of the mind and slam the door shut, hoping that will be the end of them. It never is, because the mind remembers this closetful of fear and begins the runaway process of multiplying these threats until you reach a state of hysteria. And with a mind full of unexamined fear, you have no way of knowing whether those warnings of doom are true. The end of baseless fear begins when you open the windows of your mind and expose it to the light of reason.

TRY THIS . . .

Acknowledge and examine your fear each time it arrives, and then determine its validity. If your examination finds the fear unfounded, toss it in the trash. If you aren't sure, examine the fear more carefully, even if other people consider this silly. This validity check will determine whether you should discard the fear or whether you have a problem that needs correcting. Depending on the situation, there are many ways to check fear for validity, but a good place to begin is by talking openly with your spouse, a trusted friend, or your therapist.

10
SOLUTION

WHEN SLEEP WON'T COME

How do you like to go up in a swing,
Up in the air so blue?
Oh, I do think it the pleasantest thing
Ever a child can do!

I remember sitting on my mother's lap and begging her to read, over and over, those words from Robert L. Stevenson's book, A Child's Garden of Verses. But I doubt whether Stevenson ever expected adults like me to be reciting his poems, almost a hundred years later, to lull themselves to sleep.

Last night I recited, over and over, a half dozen of my favorite childhood poems before finally dozing off to sleep. I could visualize images of myself swinging up and over those moss-covered walls and seeing the brown roofs below. These are the images that Stevenson so wondrously portrays in his poem, "The Swing." The discovery I've made is that my mind cannot focus on two different thoughts at the same time. So reciting simple repetitious poetry leaves no room for the *negative thoughts that invariably try to seep into my mind in that half-awake state between consciousness and sleep.*

Hanging onto the joys of my childhood helps to reconnect my mind to wonder and keep depression at bay. Some people might think me a bit loony, reciting children's poetry, but it works for me, and I'm committed to using anything that works in my struggle with depression.

THINGS TO CONSIDER

Insomnia can compound your depression by leaving you tired and unable to cope with even the simplest tasks. Difficulty getting to sleep and/or staying asleep is common among depression sufferers. Even *worrying* about sleep problems can detract from your well-being and hinder your recovery. Before you try other solutions, you should begin with a visit to your doctor to rule out the possibility that medication may be affecting your sleep.

There are many remedies for securing a good night's sleep, so investigate until you find those that appeal to you. The solution offered below uses the imagery and repetition of children's poetry to help you fall asleep at night. It's worth a try because of the wonderful way it transports you to a state of sleep by recapturing a bit of the child within you while separating you from the cares of the day. It's an idea that requires little effort or risk, yet offers the potential of significant rewards.

Actually, if you choose to try this idea, you are not limited to children's poetry. You can recite anything that's simple and appealing enough to take your mind away from the difficulties of your day.

TRY THIS . . .

Find a notebook and jot down a few simple lines of children's poetry, Dr. Seuss, a favorite song, a Bible verse, or whatever conjures up pleasant thoughts and images. Next, memorize these words and when you go to bed tonight, be ready to recite them over and over until you drift off to dreamland.

11
SOLUTION

FOCUS ON THE BENEFITS

— From My Journal —

I'm really getting tired of all this depression therapy. I'm tired of trying to straighten out my thinking, tired of trying to drag myself around when I've got no energy, tired of doing things I don't want to do, and tired of going places I don't really want to go to.

In some ways, this battle with depression reminds me of when I was a kid and my brother Ralph and I used to do housecleaning. We were about twelve, and the rich neighbor ladies across the road asked if my brother and I would like to earn some extra money. We usually jumped at almost any offer—but housecleaning? It sounded so sissified that we wanted to say no, but we were desperate for money.

We began by moving the stove and refrigerator, then got down on our hands and knees and scrubbed the kitchen floor. We climbed the ladder to clean the high light fixtures, replaced the bulbs and did pretty much everything the ladies wouldn't do themselves. They paid us royally when we finished. We thought that was the end of our housecleaning work, except our neighbor's friends began calling my mother and asking if the boys could help them with their house-cleaning. So we began the housecleaning tour all across town.

The only problem was that when our friends got wind of our housecleaning work, the teasing began. The "cleaning ladies," they tagged us, but we did our best to ignore them because we had a goal: saving for new bicycles.

I'll never forget the day we showed off our new bikes. We felt like the rich kids in the neighborhood for a change. The work and teasing we endured about housecleaning seemed like nothing compared to the joy of wheeling our new bikes around the neighborhood. I'm hoping my efforts to crowd out depression will end up the same way.

THINGS TO CONSIDER

There will always come days when you doubt whether your battle to eliminate depression is worth the price you're paying. Therapy can be disruptive and difficult. It can feel like it goes on forever while you question whether you're even moving toward recovery. And while you struggle with your therapy, depression will be trying to convince you that it's easier just to give in to this illness and accept the consequences it offers.

There will be other times when you feel like you have made great progress in your depression trial only to slip back into the shadows again. It's an up-and-down battle, played out again and again, devastating you each time these dark clouds return. Finding the strength to continue is a struggle and you can't help wondering if you're ever going to get back to normal.

The reality is that most of life's worthwhile things come with price tags, and therapy (and all the efforts that flow from it) is the price of solving your depression problems. You must plant this truth firmly in your mind, recognizing even in the worst of times that this is the route back to wholeness. And no matter what price you pay, when your mind's distortion is gone and clear thinking returns, your pain will turn to pride, the rewards well worth the high price you've paid.

TRY THIS . . .

On a sheet of notebook paper or a page in your journal, draw a vertical line down the center. On the left side, list the various therapies you have used, or plan to use, to lessen your depression. On the right side, list the benefits you expect to receive when clear thinking is restored. This exercise will help you understand that the benefits of depression therapy far outweigh the effort required.

FORGIVE AND . . .

W hy do I keep returning to my youth to single out those traumatic memories that I can never change?

There was the Friday evening when our family started out for my
Uncle Clair's home, two hundred miles away. My dad had been
secretly drinking before we left home, and after about an hour on the
road, he became too drunk to continue driving. Mom took the keys
but, since she didn't know how to drive, all six of us spent a freez-
ing night huddled in our car, parked on the roadside.

I'm still shamefully embarrassed when I think about the many
occasions when my mother made me wear my sister's underwear to
bed because I had wet the sheets the night before. Words can never
describe the humiliation I felt.

And still vivid in my mind is the time my mother caught me, a first
grader, walking through mud puddles in our driveway. My punish-
ment was being locked in our old Ford station wagon that evening
while the rest of the family went to the county fair. I can still feel the
terror of seeing them walk away, leaving me all alone in the car.
Those two or three hours seemed like a lifetime.

But why? Why have I kept returning, over and over, to those painful memories, as if that's all there were? Perhaps I convinced myself that I could absolve my own inadequacies by blaming my parents. I can finally see that my own thinking was twisted and I realize that no matter how wrong or grievous these childhood episodes may have been, they don't negate the love my mother and father had for me. Perfect parents? Not by a long shot, but learning to trade blame for forgiveness has helped erase the scars from my own heart.

THINGS TO CONSIDER

Forgiveness is not so much about forgetting as it is about remembering . . . remembering that we are all human, prone to mistakes, and lacking perfection. You need to understand that seeking perfection for yourself or others is the most imperfect quest of all. You need to remind yourself that we are all sojourners on the road of life, and we all try to do the best we can with what life has given us. Accepting others in spite of their faults and prejudices is *the* prerequisite for accepting ourselves. Forgiveness, like love, must begin with forgiving yourself before it can be offered to others.

Many things about life offer you no choice. You did not choose blue eyes or the circumstances of your birth. You certainly did not choose depression. But holding grudges, feeling resentment, and seeking revenge *are* your choices. These things can seem so sweet and satisfying until you realize that they're drowning you, adding to your depression. Your recovery can only begin when you accept life, imperfections and all, and know that you are privileged just to be alive.

TRY THIS . . .

Use a page of your journal to make a list of the people who you need to forgive, including yourself. As you write each name, first remember that person's many good qualities, then release all the anger and resentment you hold toward him or her by the act of forgiveness.

NOTE: You may want to make the forgiveness page a permanent part of your journal because you will likely need it often. Remember that it's okay to forgive the same person many times.

13
SOLUTION

TRADE DOUBTS FOR DREAMS

— FROM MY JOURNAL —

A ridiculous thought keeps popping up in my head these past few weeks: the idea that I should write a book about my battle with depression. I keep pushing the idea aside—I know how tough it is to write a book, and who am I to write about depression? All I know is the agony I've been through in this fight to restore my mind. But write a book about it? I don't think so.

Still, I will always remember the first thing I looked for when depression slammed into my life—someone who had fought and won their battle with depression, someone who could tell me what it was like, what to expect, and how to beat it.

My initial encounter with depression was a long time ago and although I sometimes feel like I've been through hell, I'm finally close enough to see the sunlight shining into the far end of the tunnel. When I think about it, I've become the person that I yearned to find back at the beginning. I not only know the torment of this illness; at last I'm finding the pathway of recovery. Living in depression's trenches has taught me a lot, and none of it theoretical.

Maybe I should write that book; writing another book is on my forgotten dream list. Maybe I could help erase the stigma of this illness and support others facing a similar ordeal. I could offer the one thing depressed people seek most—a spark of light to illuminate the darkness of depression.

AUTHOR'S NOTE: *I began this book one day at three in the morning when sleep eluded me. I wanted to convey the truthful message that depression is a bitch, but you can find your way back to wholeness if you're willing to fight. In spite of the length and difficulty of my own struggle, I still believe that's true.*

THINGS TO CONSIDER

Depression and dreams don't mix well. Pursuing a dream has the power to crowd the doubts of depression out of your life. Most people have "forgotten" dreams tucked away somewhere in the recesses of their mind, dreams they've given up on or put aside while waiting for the right opportunity to come along. Now might be a good time to search through those forgotten dreams to find one that makes you vibrate with excitement. If you're lucky, you have an idea that can rekindle the passion of your soul so deeply that no room is left for the blues. It may be a hazy vision from the past that time has now defined in greater detail. Or it may be a recent idea that you have been pushing away with excuses that lack validity. How about the rock garden along the hillside that you've talked so much about, the getaway cabin in the woods that you've always wanted to build, the puppet theater in your garage where you would make hand puppets and teach neighbor children puppetry?

Maybe now is the time to let your dream become the key to unlock a passion so deep it will stir your soul, a dream so encompassing that it leaves no time, no room, and no place for depression in your life. There's no need to dive off the deep end to begin this journey. A few small steps in the direction of your dream will start you on your way.

TRY THIS . . .

Begin with a list of your dreams and keep narrowing it down to the one that's powerful enough to ignite your soul. If you can't start the project, then *write* about it in your journal. Expound on every aspect of this idea and push aside your fears and doubts; search for ways to make it come true. Every dream begins with the first step—so take it now.

NONSENSE MAKES PERFECT SENSE

— From My Journal —

O ur three grandsons arrived yesterday for the long weekend. Ordinarily I would have rejoiced at the news, but depression really has me dragging lately. I begged off from a shopping trip today, consenting instead to stay home and look after the boys. Little Colin, the youngest, wanted to paint pictures, so I spread some newspapers on the floor in the den, got out the finger paints, and put my young artist to work in an old shirt of mine. Then I headed out to the big silver maple by the deck where the two older boys were already spinning each other in the tire swing.

After a few minutes of pushing the tire swing, I figured I'd better go check on my four-year-old "Rembrandt." As I started up the stairs to the den, Muffy, our white kitten, went streaking by and a quick glimpse revealed she had a badly bleeding ear. I took off after her and finally caught her in the basement, and I was surprised to find that the red blood I'd seen was really red paint. It didn't take much detective work to figure out that little Colin had been painting the cat. One ear was red, the other blue, and the rest of the cat was a rainbow of smeared colors. I quickly headed back up to the den to confront my young artist.

"Did you do that?" I asked, "Paint the cat?"

I thought he would deny it but instead he proudly claimed the cat was now an astronaut. I tried to have a serious little chat but the conversation was so innocently hilarious that I had to cover my mouth to keep from exploding with laughter.

Depression? What depression? Humor is almost like a magic wand that can make me totally forget that ugly word.

THINGS TO CONSIDER

Humor is a marvelous device to boost sagging spirits. It comes in many forms, ranging from simple jokes to elaborate gags and simply seeing the funny side of things. The depth of your sense of humor depends on the lens with which you view life. Some people develop this comic lens in childhood, enabling them to see almost anything in a humorous light. Others live a lifetime almost devoid of humor. Humor is a dimension of life worth cultivating because it has the power to ease the pain and melancholy of depression.

How do you train yourself to see the funny side of life? Often, it's learned from fun-loving people around you who are able to laugh *at* themselves and *with* others. You can learn it from reading books and watching television shows that embrace the lighter side of life. You can learn it by paying close attention to the funny antics of innocent children, who are absolute experts at the joy of nonsense. Practice laughing at yourself and let life amuse you with its absurdities.

TRY THIS . . .

Think about ways you could increase the amount of humor you see in daily life and record these in your journal. That done, look for opportunities to make others laugh and add these to your list. Make sure to notice each time you catch yourself laughing out loud: That's the reward.

15
SOLUTION

LET MUSIC LIFT YOUR SOUL

— FROM MY JOURNAL —

I strolled down the terrace steps into the back yard this morning, singing "What a Wonderful World." The problem was that I failed to see my next-door neighbor puttering around on the other side of the shrubs. I hadn't quite made it to the garden shed when I saw him part the branches and stick his face through my evergreen hedge.

"That was a great rendition," he hollered over, half laughing.

At first I was a little embarrassed as I walked over to the hedge to chat. Our conversation was mostly about last night's storm, the dogwood blossoms, and the upcoming school budget. He was kind enough not to mention my song again and we soon parted ways and got back to our respective chores.

The truth is I love to sing. Belting out a few lines of a favorite song can lift my low spirits to the sky, and that's not because I have any musical talent. In fact Mr. Mulaney, my fourth-grade music teacher, refused to let me sing with the class because he said I threw everyone else off key.

It's surprising that my year with Mr. Mulaney never dampened my

43

love of singing or my enjoyment of many types of music. The right vocal or instrumental can touch my soul like nothing else can. I admit my musical knowledge may be limited, but maybe in my next life I'll have the talent to be a musician—who knows? I do know one thing about music though: You don't have to be a good singer to love singing.

THINGS TO CONSIDER

Although most of us have our favorite recording artists and our preferred types and styles of music, we still may fail to understand the power of music to enrich our lives. Often we forget to take full advantage of the most obvious depression fighting resources around us—music is one such resource. Whether you prefer rock, country, classical, pop, hip-hop or gospel, all have the power to transform our lives by leaving our cares far behind. Few therapies are as effective or as enjoyable as music in all of its many forms. How about some new music and perhaps a new music player to take along on your walks or listen to while you garden or work in the yard?

And if you enjoy singing, then make it a habit to sing while you work. Planting a song in your heart and on your lips has the power to lift you out of the doldrums and move you to the sunny side of the street. How good do you have to be to enjoy singing, or even humming, for that matter? The truth is that it's not the quality of your voice but the joy in your heart that creates a happy feeling.

Maybe you've always wanted to learn to play the piano, the guitar, or something else. Do it—do it now, without worrying about whether you have talent. Find a way to make music thrive in your life.

TRY THIS . . .

Learn all the lyrics to three of the songs you most love to sing. Then remind yourself to sing at least a few lines from this music every day. Sing along with the music playing on your car radio, stereo, or portable MP3 player. If your neighbor, spouse, or the driver stopped beside you at the traffic light looks at you like you're crazy—just keep singing.

16

CONFIDE IN A FRIEND

— FROM MY JOURNAL —

I don't know what came over me but yesterday, for the first time, I confided in a friend about my depression. I've known Margie for years and it's common knowledge that her husband, Rob, suffers from this illness also. I, on the other hand, have treated my own ordeal more like a military secret. I'm not proud of this but having people shun me, exclude me, and gossip about me has always seemed too big a price to pay for candor.

Anyway, I happened to sit next to Margie last night at the Mission Committee meeting and when I inquired about Rob, the weariness in her voice belied her words. I understood, too well, the strain she must be under trying to hold things together. As the meeting ended, I leaned over to her and asked her to stay a few minutes, saying that I had something I wanted to discuss. When the room emptied I closed the door and pulled up a chair.

"I think you and Rob should know that I'm battling depression, too...." I tried to continue but Margie stared at me in disbelief. I could see the tears sliding from the corner of her eye as she looked *away and began digging a tissue out of her purse. I immediately regretted that I had broached the subject.*

After a minute or two, Margie turned back toward me, fighting to regain her composure. "Dick, I can't believe what you're telling me. You?—You have depression? You always seem so . . . so optimistic, so positive about everything."

We talked quite a while last night . . . about doctors, and treatments, and medications . . . about the isolation and loneliness of depression. We also talked about hope and better times ahead. It was an uplifting step for me, one I should have taken long before.

Things to Consider

Many people who suffer depression don't have a supportive friend who truly understands and cares about them. But if you're fortunate enough to have such a relationship, it can add strength and comfort to your battle. If you're still looking for such a friend, be careful whom you choose, because not everyone has the empathy and patience to help you. Good intentions alone aren't enough for this sustaining role. In fact, you might be better off with no one rather than someone who constantly provides negative input.

The person you choose for support may be a family member, a current friend, or someone who has faced similar problems.

Whoever it is, patient listening and confidentiality are essential. Advice from a friend should usually be offered only when sought and even then, tempered with sensitivity.

Simply asking someone you already know for their help is a rather direct approach that often works. Expressing your thanks to people who currently support you may encourage them to continue or even expand their efforts. However you choose to pursue it, you need to remain open to the possibility of close friendship and do your part to foster such relationships.

TRY THIS . . .

Think about the people you know who may have the needed qualities to become a supportive friend. Think also about ways that you might approach them to explore such possibilities of friendship. Many people, if not most, would consider your willingness to trust and confide in them a great compliment.

Now prepare a list of several people who you would consider for this role of friend and decide how to approach them. If your efforts lead to friendships with more than one person, that's even better.

17

SOLUTION

PRETEND YOU'RE OKAY

— From My Journal —

*E*ven before we got home from our Ohio vacation last Tuesday, I could feel myself slipping into a quagmire of gloom and worry. Doubt was seeping into the situations I had previously felt so positive about. It seemed almost as if someone had smeared mud on my glasses, leaving me with a murky view of everything. It devastates me that my outlook can so quickly reverse and, for no apparent reason, let me slide into a funk like this.

Then something surprising happened the day after I got home. My old buddy Bruce dropped in (unexpected, and I might add, unwelcome, because I wasn't in the mood for company) with a basket of tomatoes from his garden. I've never told Bruce about my bouts with depression, so I felt obliged to act as if I were feeling fine. He went on with his usual chatter about the garden, his grandkids, and the same lame jokes I've heard a dozen times before. I pretended to laugh and appear interested as he rambled on. The surprising part was that even though I had begun by faking my interest, I slowly found myself being drawn into a real conversation. As we tossed our usual insults back and forth, my mood improved and I began to feel much better.

When Bruce left an hour or so later, my energy level had increased considerably, so I decided to go out to the back yard and finish painting the tool shed, a task that I had started over a week before. I was a different person for the rest of the day.

My visit with Bruce taught me a valuable lesson about fighting depression. Pretending I'm okay can somehow make me okay. It seems silly, I know, but it really does work that way.

THINGS TO CONSIDER

At first glance, some tactics that could help you defeat depression might seem counterintuitive, or too simple to really work. Acting like you're okay when you're not is one of those tricks. It's an idea that may surprise you with positive results.

Sometimes the situation calls for this behavior: You have to act "normal" in front of other people when you feel depressed. Hard as it may be, embrace the opportunity and watch what happens.

It also works when you're alone. The next time you find yourself slipping into the shadow of depression, find any trivial task or project that you've been thinking about and dig in before you have time to change your mind. Make it something modest like watering the flowers, reorganizing your spice rack, or washing your truck windows. The surprising thing is that by the time you've finished this minor task, you may find you have enough energy to move on to bigger projects, and even if you don't, at least you'll feel better for having accomplished something.

The key to all this may be the act of talking, or physical movement itself. Whatever the case, getting active and/or projecting a positive attitude or energy (no matter how little you feel like doing so) becomes its own wonderful, self-fulfilling prophecy.

TRY THIS . . .

There are many opportunities in which you can try out the pretending game, perhaps at dinner tonight, the supermarket, the hair salon, or maybe with your colleagues at work. It's worth a try at home, too, even when you're alone. In your journal, make a list of three places where you would be willing to test the *pretending* idea. Then try it and see if it works for you.

TALK BACK TO YOUR BEAST

— FROM MY JOURNAL —

"**B**ack talk" was one guaranteed way of getting into trouble with my mother. No matter our reason, she did not tolerate any kind of talking back from us kids. "Just walk away" was her solution. Still, I find it tough just walking away from the malicious lies that this depression beast keeps telling me. Haven't I put up with these insults about my character and intelligence long enough?

I had a fitful sleep last night, tormented by a disturbing dream that someone had ransacked our office. In my dream, I was the bumbling imbecile who forgot to lock the door when I left. Finally, around four in the morning, I gave up trying to sleep and came down here, sinking into my chair by the window. The warmed-up coffee tastes good and awakens me enough to understand, once more, that my problems are all part of this disgusting game that depression is playing with my mind. It's an entrapping game that could be called "Tricks and Deception," in which the goal is to see how many devious lies this depression bully can convince me are true.

Do I know better than to fall for these tricks? Of course I do. I'm not the wimp this depression beast thinks I am, and it's time for me to stop being suckered by his scornful lies. Next time he taunts me with, "you're losing it," I plan to send it right back at him, just like I did when I was a kid. Maybe I'm too old for the "Liar, liar, pants on fire" response I used back then, but I'll shout something to let him know that I'm not buying that garbage anymore.

Sorry, Mom. Sometimes you can't just walk away.

Things to Consider

As you've searched for ways to reduce depression, you've probably discovered that talking to yourself really can plant positive ideas in your mind. Now you may be surprised to find there is another type of self-talk that can also be effective for combating depression. With this tactic you talk back directly at your symbolic depression "beast," using whatever name you prefer (Winston Churchill named his depression the "Black Dog").

What do you say to the beast? Maybe that you know it's trying to distort your thinking, that it may as well take its deceit and head down the highway because you're not about to let it ruin your life. Say whatever you feel like saying—let your frustrations and feelings pour out in a torrent (using words as explicit as required!).

Another benefit of this therapy is that giving your depression a name helps to separate you from your illness. It's not you, and you're not it. Depression may be hounding you, but it's not a *part* of you. And talking back to your vile beast allows you to exhaust your frustration instead of allowing it to fester in your mind.

How ridiculous is the idea of taking your wrath out on a symbolic depression beast? Not nearly as ridiculous as berating yourself.

TRY THIS . . .

> Give your depression a name that reminds you of the tormenting characteristics of this illness: Rascal, Dr. Evil, Pig, Ogre, Beast, or something much saltier and more colorful. Make the nickname match your hatred of the illness.
>
> Write down the name you chose in your journal as a reminder that you and your depression are not the same thing. Think about what you might say to your beast, and when the time's right, say it!

19
SOLUTION

STRENGTHEN YOUR FAITH

— FROM MY JOURNAL —

Worry is a big part of depression, and I seem to spend half of my time worrying about something—something that never happens. I think about the hours lost and the countless times I've made myself, and often others, miserable simply by anticipating troubles that never came.

Last week, while vacationing in Vermont, Anita and I happened onto one of those picturesque little New England churches so often seen on magazine covers. It was Sunday morning, so we decided to drop in for the worship service. An elderly, gray-haired lady with rough, knobby hands was sitting at an old upright piano, pounding out music so glorious that it would've thrilled even the Carnegie Hall crowd. We slid into a rear pew where we could look out the tall gothic windows toward the magnificent Green Mountains beyond. I couldn't help but wonder how much closer anyone could get to heaven than this. No game of hide and seek was required to find my Maker in that divine setting.

I confess that I was too busy daydreaming about God's magnificent landscape that morning to remember much of what the preacher had to say. But later, I found this humorous little note on the last page of the church bulletin: "Don't tell me that worry doesn't help! I've worried about a million different things and none of them have ever happened." I first suspected that someone put it there in an effort to fill up extra space. Yet the words struck a chord of such undeniable truth in my life that I began to wonder if God Himself had placed it there, just for me.

THINGS TO CONSIDER

Prayers are too often like one-sided telephone conversations. You rattle off your needs but fail to listen for God's answer. The clatter of everyday life drowns out the voice of God and all the while you complain that He's not listening. If you're waiting for an e-mail or a phone call—God doesn't do those. Don't be surprised to find Him at unexpected times and places. His answer to your prayer may reveal itself in an article you're reading, pop into your head while you're mowing the lawn, or be manifested in any of a thousand other ways.

To find the answers God has for your life, you must first find God. Listen for Him in the rustling of the grass, the singing of the wren, the crackle of the fire. See Him in a meadow laden with wildflowers or among the shooting stars on a summer night. He is infinite and He is everywhere.

Is this God stuff for real, you may wonder, or is it just a giant hoax perpetrated on mankind? Only you can decide, but if you choose to *believe,* you will find yourself in the company of Einstein, Gandhi, Marie Curie and countless others who have found strength and comfort in various forms of the Almighty.

TRY THIS . . .

> If you desire religious faith to be part of your solution for depression, begin by preparing a list of resources that could help you strengthen your faith. One by one, pursue each resource on your list.

LONELY, BUT NOT ALONE

— From My Journal —

Another note from Anita

Hi Dick,

From the porch window, I can see you out there raking leaves. The way you're moving, I can tell you're a little low. I'm sorry that yesterday was such a rough day for you—is there anything I can do to help?

I'm writing you this note because I wanted to answer the question you asked me last night. . . . Yes, I do know what it's like to feel lonely. And I understand how you can be lonely even when you're surrounded by a roomful of people. Sometimes when you're sitting right next to me, I can tell your thoughts are far away. Feelings like this happen to all of us, but depression escalates them to a level that I probably can't imagine. We often think we do, but none of us really knows how someone else feels. Do I know what my loneliness feels like? Of course I do, but quite honestly, I can only guess about yours.

It's hard to get past the whys. Why do bad things sometimes happen to good people? Look at Maggie—she's a saint, but I don't know if she will ever walk again, and Rodger Gertz, he's still laid up from that heart surgery last spring; the bank is not the same without him. I guess life is a bit like the roulette wheel—we all take our chances and it seems like most everyone lands on a bad place sooner or later.

When you're up to it, let's try some new things like taking a few day-trips with the kids. Walking the canal bank might be fun. And you know the kids would love to help you build a new dog house for Brassie. The joys of life are still there but a little harder to grasp these days.

Love,
Anita

THINGS TO CONSIDER

Depression has a way of isolating us and leaving us with a sense of dejection. We can be surrounded by a group of friends and this feeling of isolation slips into our senses to drain away our positive feelings. Suddenly we feel lost, like no one cares, and we're on our own. Strangely, these weird feelings occur even while someone we love is standing at our side. It's another of depression's sneaky symptoms that tries to flip-flop the truth and trick us into thinking we are forsaken. Unfortunately, there is no easy solution for solving this loneliness except to surround yourself with people who care and to stay involved in life.

Another solution is to refute the voice that answers "No!" every time someone suggests or invites you to participate in something. Shove aside your reluctance and join in; most of the time you will be glad you did, and even if you don't have a great time, it's probably still better than spending the day wishing you had said yes instead of no.

TRY THIS . . .

Prepare a list of activities that involve people you enjoy. These can be purely imaginary, at least for the moment . . . just little things like having lunch with a friend, holding a joint garage sale with your neighbor, taking the kids to a funny movie. Then, when and if you can, invite others to *do* these things.

You may find that charitable activities are doubly satisfying. The local theater groups can almost always use an extra hand with the props and scenery, and almost every kid's sports team can use an assistant coach or manager.

21
SOLUTION

MAKE GRATITUDE A HABIT

— From My Journal —

*I*t's almost three in the morning, as I write this. I should be upstairs asleep but instead I'm here in my chair on the back porch again. I've been chased out of bed by that same old futile question, Why me? Why did this dreadful depression stuff have to happen to me?

My grogginess of being half asleep is dissipating now and I'm beginning to think more rationally. On the wall directly in front of my chair is a large photo of our family. The part I always zoom in on first is my four grinning grandkids; how easily they can bribe me with those great smiles. My eyes move up to the other faces in the photo: a son, a daughter, their spouses, and the greatest wife in the world.

I could never forget that fateful day, half a lifetime ago, when I stopped to help three girls stranded along the highway when their car quit. One of them became my bride and thus began a lifetime commitment to each other. And I can still feel that shiver of fatherly pride seeing Jeff walk up the aisle at Duke University to receive his master's degree, still feel the thrill of watching Nancy and her golden retriever eliminate the competition, one by one, to become state champions at the New York State Fair. And how about the day Alex scored a bases-loaded home run to win that Little League game? How many grandfathers can top that one?

I can't deny that I've known my share of bad things, too, including this battle with depression. Still, if I am going to ask, "Why me?" regarding the bad stuff, wouldn't I also have to ask why I've been so richly blessed in other ways?

Things to Consider

One of the ways that depression keeps you down is by convincing you that everything about your life is miserable and that you have nothing to be thankful for. The truth is that everyone has ups and downs, but if you examine your life accurately, you'll likely find dozens of things to be thankful for. Depression causes us to feel sorry for ourselves by focusing our minds only on what is wrong. *Why me? Why me? Why me?* is a useless refrain that can never move you toward recovery.

The best way to stop sloshing around in self-pity is by learning to show gratitude for the many fortunate things about your life. Have you thanked your family, friends, and others who support you? Are you appreciative of a sunny morning with birds chirping outside your window? Your faithful dog, a hobby you love, or the hundreds of other benefits that you're privileged to enjoy? Expect good things to happen in your life and think often about how fortunate you are to be so richly blessed. Then make a habit of offering thanks to everyone who helps you.

Try This . . .

Write down in your journal a list of five ways to show your gratitude for help received from others, perhaps a thank-you note to someone who has assisted you, a prayer of gratefulness for a good night's sleep, a hug for a child you love. Place a check next to the item on your list each time you remember to say "thanks," because each instance is an accomplishment for you. Continue this, constantly adding new names to your list, until gratitude becomes a habit.

22

WALK ON THE WILD SIDE

— FROM MY JOURNAL —

I could feel the day bearing down on me this afternoon. It was almost as if someone were dimming the lights while I tried to reduce the piles of paperwork on my desk. I stepped outside, hoping the fresh air would help clear my mind.

In back of our office, a quarter mile or more away, is an undeveloped wooded area, and almost without thinking, I headed there. Walking deep into the woods, I came upon a fallen tree and sat down to rest. Beside me was a small clearing where the mottled sun danced each time the breeze fluttered through the leaves. Two gray squirrels were chasing each other up and down the branches of a nearby sycamore like children playing tag. The longer I sat there, the more relaxed I became, as the melodic sounds of nature blended together like a hushed rhapsody, quieting my mind and soothing my soul. I began to wonder how this woodland, which seemed so unplanned, could abound in such beauty and harmony. At first I felt like an intruder who had snuck into a place where I didn't belong. But the gentle voices of that idyllic setting whispered to my mind, inviting me to join the cast of nature's great drama. Slowly I began to understand that all living things have assigned places on the stage of life and that my role is not to orchestrate the world, but to play me and find contentment in my own part.

Too soon it was time to go. People would be wondering where I was. Walking back, I felt like Mother Nature had gently kneaded her healing balm deep into my depressive wounds to soothe my twisted thinking. I already know that one session with this therapist won't be enough: I'm going back as soon as I can to find my special place among the singing birds and tangled trees.

Things to Consider

There is a tonic to ease the pain of depression; it's called nature. A dose is waiting for you in the nearest woods or beside some remote stream. Hike in and find your seat on a flat rock or tree stump, and experience a fascinating show of timeless magic. Feel the cool breeze as it tosses the branches about the billowy sky. Hear the song of the birds and the babble of the brook combine to form a symphony that even Beethoven could never write. Sing, pray, meditate, contemplate, whatever satisfies your soul. Let go and lose yourself in this fascinating place where time is measured by daylight and darkness, not clocks.

When dusk arrives, play the old game of wishing on the first star you see. And how about a little chat with the moon-man, if it's not his night off? Observe how perfectly nature has arranged every detail of this magnificent masterpiece. Before you leave, give thanks for this serene place and for your life. Take with you all the rapture that your heart can hold, and return often for a refill.

Try This . . .

Make a list of potential places where you can leave the hassle of your daily life behind and commune with nature. Commit to explore at least one of them this week. Sense a new and deeper peace as you discover the quiet peace and timeless patience surrounding you. Visit often, letting nature provide the comfort and restoration you seek.

23
SOLUTION

LIVE YOUR LIFE OVER

What if I had my life to live over? *That's a question I often ponder. Thinking back to the time my son's friend was killed in an auto accident, in the midst of our grief we could not help but speculate about how minor changes that day could have eliminated this tragedy. If only he had taken a different way home, driven a different car or did this or did that. Yet we all know that life has only forward gears; we never get that chance to go back and try again.*

Still, these questions about living my life over have haunted me all day. How would I do things differently if I had another chance? What would I keep and what would I eliminate? Drawn deep into this mental speculation, I found myself visualizing time machines from science-fiction movies and wishing they were real, wishing I could go back and redo at least parts of my past.

I'd just about pushed these weird thoughts out of my head tonight when an even crazier question popped up. Is it really too late to make those live-my-life-over changes? I can't undo the past but I can still alter my future by rearranging the priorities of my life. There are wrongs in my life that can still be righted, misunderstandings that are not too late to correct. There's forgiveness needed and relationships I can rebuild. Maybe I can even find some of that lost exuberance from my youthful days when I chased dreams and fully embraced life. Surely I can find a better way.

Things to Consider

Many people, regardless of age, are inclined to think it's too late to make meaningful alterations to their lives. They may not like where they live or the job they hold. They may not like the people they associate with or the person they have become. Still they're reluctant to risk change. Often you hear people say something like, "That's just the way I am," or, "I can't help it if I act that way." Fear of failing is the reason most people resist the changes they would like to make.

Depression lowers your confidence and increases your doubt, which prevents you from becoming the person you'd really like to be. Depression exaggerates the dangers of improving your life by warning you that you're too old, too poor, too ill, too tired, too something, to make any meaningful adjustments. It makes you afraid to reach out and find the better life that's waiting for you.

The truth is that many of the changes you could make if you

had your life to live over can still be made. And a satisfying life is the sure solution for squelching the voice of depression.

TRY THIS . . .

Prepare a list of seven things that you would do differently if you had your life to life over again. Then carefully study your list and decide which of these changes are still possible and which you have the desire and determination to pursue. Next, prepare your plan and decide how and where to make the first move that leads to the person you want to become.

PLAY YOURSELF A LOVE SONG

— From My Journal —

*Y*esterday, the grandkids were visiting, and two-year-old Jacob *fell and skinned his knee while playing on the back steps. As I carried him, crying, into the house I immediately began blaming myself. You should've been watching him closer. You should've been holding his hand on the stairway. You let him get hurt. Of course Jacob was back outside playing in a matter of minutes, proudly showing off his new bandage, but I was still condemning myself hours later.*

Today at work, I had hardly got settled at my desk when I was informed that a delivery of critical supplies had been shipped to the wrong place because someone had given the trucker an incomplete address. "That had to be me," I thought. "I really screwed up." I continued to insult myself the rest of the morning with words like stupid and inept until my secretary finally dug out the purchase order to make corrections and found it had been signed by someone else—not me.

If the insults I used on myself earlier this morning had been directed toward anyone but me, I would certainly have apologized

once I knew the truth. Instead, my mind sent out a new torrent of mental accusations berating me for believing that the error was my fault in the first place. I give up. There's no way to win when I'm in one of these beat-myself-up moods.

Business has taught me to expect a little personal abuse now and then, but it's a lot tougher to handle when the perpetrator is me.

THINGS TO CONSIDER

Who is the person who most often hurts you with cruel lies and distorted truths? You may be surprised to find that it's you. Can you recall a day when things seemed to be going okay and then, *wham!*—you made a simple mistake and began berating yourself with words like *dumb* and *numbskull*? You likely continued filling your mind with such disparaging phrases as, *I never get it right*, or, *I don't know how to do anything.*

It's difficult to understand why anyone would belittle himself or herself, but persons afflicted with depression often have that inclination. It's almost like there's a song titled "You're a Stupid Jerk" that begins playing in your head before you have a chance to make your own selection. That song steals your self-confidence and drives you deeper into the doldrums. It's essential to understand that you don't have to participate in such damaging rhetoric. At those first repulsive words, you must learn to hit that mental *stop button*. The faster you're able to stop these mind-trashing messages, the faster you return to logical thinking.

Why not learn a new song, a song that extols your many virtues and talents and ignores your shortcomings and mistakes, a love song that fills your mind with the hope and promise of a brighter today and a better tomorrow?

Try This . . .

> Divide a sheet of notebook paper in half vertically and on the left side, list some of the mean, insulting words you've recently used to berate yourself. Then on the right side, list the positive, uplifting words you should have used. Resolve to stop beating up on yourself in the future and focus your blame on the beast of depression, where it belongs.

25

DO SOMETHING!

— FROM MY JOURNAL —

I'*ve sat here half the evening watching TV, without really caring enough to even change the channel. I'm tired, too tired to even move. What little energy I have is consumed by worry, about my granddaughter's speech problems, about whether I'll have enough money for retirement, even about tomorrow's weather. I can hear those taunting tapes playing in my head again. They're reeling off their usual predictions of doom, but I'm too paralyzed to even care about it.*

Anita jolts me out of my stupor by asking if I would hang a picture for her. I start to complain that I'm too tired. Yet I can't help but remember how staunchly she has stood by me through this whole depression ordeal. Still moaning, I finally get out of my chair to find a hammer and the other stuff I need. By then she's pointing to three pictures she wants hung. A flash of anger shoots through me and I'm about to protest, but she's already smiling and thanking me so I can hardly refuse.

The amazing thing about those few minutes I spent hanging her pictures tonight is the momentum they provided to carry me on to other projects. I got a ladder and replaced the bulb in the lamppost. My workbench in the garage hadn't been straightened up for months; I tackled that. As I finished each task, I could sense my energy level rising and I felt more like my old self, right up to bedtime.

Thinking back, I realize that I probably would have vegetated in front of that TV for the rest of the evening if Anita's picture hanging project hadn't got me up and going. I'm beginning to figure out that getting myself out of this blue funk often begins with getting out of my cushy chair.

Things to Consider

Sometimes your favorite chair provides a comforting oasis to sort out the distortions of your thinking so you can restore clarity to your mind. More likely though, the cushy chair will entice you to sit for hours while your internal dialogue of self-denigration sinks you deeper into a state of malaise. Isolation and inactivity support a depressive mood. An important maxim for solving this mood illness is *Do Something*. Almost any worthwhile activity helps to elevate your state of mind and build the momentum needed to keep you in a positive frame of mind. In choosing your activities, look for things that offer a sense of achievement without excessive frustration. A couple of ways to do this is to break your projects into smaller parts and refrain from unnecessary deadlines.

Remind yourself the next time you sink deep into the cushions of your favorite couch or chair: *Don't stay here too long.* As astounding as it may seem, just getting up and doing something may be the best depression medicine of all.

TRY THIS . . .

Prepare a list of activities that help divert you from the clutches of depression: mowing the lawn, a trip to the flea market, photographing wildflowers—any of the active things you love to do. Keep this list handy and next time you get trapped in the soft folds of your favorite chair, pull out your list, select an activity, and get yourself moving in a positive direction.

DEVELOP A STRATEGY

— From My Journal —

my current bout with depression has plagued me for several weeks now, but I keep going. What else can I do? Motivation has deserted me so that even the smallest task requires a Herculean effort. I've spent the last hour just trying to find the energy to get out of this chair and walk to the mailbox. My mind keeps telling me that I'm too tired, and that the mail is probably bad news anyway. Why I pay any attention to this babble I'll never understand, but I do.

I'm aware that my thinking has become convoluted but where these illogical thoughts come from I have no idea. They're not mine, that's for sure. I've got to quit listening to this rot if I expect anything to change.

Maybe I need some sort of plan, something like the plans I've used for solving business problems. It's usually best to start by redefining the problem; with depression that's easy: distorted thinking. Most business planning requires a review of the current solutions to determine which are helpful and which are not. The next step is a search for better remedies. Ideas can come from various sources:

reading, talking with associates, or finding a specialist in the problem area. Finally, everything gets boiled down to the best remedies available, and this becomes the plan.

Maybe an approach like this won't work for depression, but I think it's worth a try. Having a plan would at least assure me that I have some sense of direction for my life. Still, I've been around the block enough times to know that a plan won't cure depression. In fact, a plan doesn't solve anything unless it's well implemented. That's where the really hard part comes in.

THINGS TO CONSIDER

Abraham Lincoln said, "It's not so much where you are that counts, but the direction you're tending to go." That's certainly true about depression, which whips you around so often that you have trouble understanding which way you're headed.

Developing a game plan to combat depression can reduce anxiety and provide assurances that you're moving in the right direction. Resources for developing your plan are all around you: books, web sites, people, etc. Begin by familiarizing yourself with the strategies, therapies, and treatments available, and then consult with your doctor or therapist about which solutions might work best for you. As you progress down the path of recovery, you will need to revise your plan from time to time by adding new ideas and eliminating those that aren't right for you. Think of your game plan as your compass; keep it adjusted, and check it often to make sure you're moving in the right direction.

A similar idea would be to prepare a depression emergency kit that contains a few pick-me-ups that can be used quickly when your mood sags without warning. Include things in your kit like a trip to the bookstore, time in the garden, a phone call to a good friend—anything that lifts your spirits.

TRY THIS . . .

Take a small notebook and label it *Game Plan*. Record in it the therapies that you find most effective for eliminating your depression. Search constantly for new therapies and, after testing them, add the best ones to your plan. Then prepare a schedule to implement these therapies and make a commitment to follow through.

DEPRESSION EMERGENCY KIT: Find a few easy-to-implement, mood-lifting ideas and write them on a small card to keep in your purse or wallet. When you feel the blues coming on, pull out the card (you can do this mentally or physically) and select an idea to help keep you on top of the situation.

27
SOLUTION

KEEP A JOURNAL

— From My Journal —

Tonight I'm rummaging through two boxes of my old journals, reading passages here and there. Until now I had been afraid to face this painful past, fearful that these written reminders might be enough to drag my mind back into that crippling darkness that haunted me for so long. But now my new confidence ignores these fears and assures me that reading these old journals will not unleash the depressive beast that decimated my past.

As I began reading, the first astonishing revelation was that it took me so long to understand and accept depression as the cause of my constant fatigue, insomnia, and digestive disorders. The stigma that associates this illness with weak and crazy people was so over-whelming that I tried vehemently to deny depression was my problem. My journal writings reveal my profound sense of hopelessness as I struggled desperately to find my old self. Looking back, I can see how my pride, the need to look and act okay, denied me the opportunity to find the help I so desperately needed. Nothing I read here *tonight surprises me now that I clearly understand the power of this illness to plant and cultivate such deceitful lies.*

I pack my old writings away with a new realization of how much they contributed to my recovery. My journal was the one place I could be totally honest. It was the place where I could confess my fears, vent my rage, or cry in despair. My journal never blabbed my secrets, offered unwanted advice, or made accusations. Sometimes I neglected my journal for weeks on end, but I was always welcomed back to write again. Perhaps more amazing than anything else was the way truth stood out in bold print once my words were placed on paper. This revelation of truth allowed me to separate myself from my illness.

THINGS TO CONSIDER

A journal is one place where you can say whatever you please. You can spill out your most private feelings about any aspect of your life, no matter how distorted or illogical they might seem to others. You can keep a journal daily, weekly, or whenever you feel like it. You can ignore it for weeks without anyone nagging at you to write, and then go back to it whenever you please.

Writing in your journal is in some ways like conversing with a caring friend, a friend who listens patiently to what you have to say instead of cutting in with unsolicited advice. A journal seems to amplify good news, while the bad news usually seems less harsh in the form of the written word. People are sometimes surprised to find that solutions to their problems bubble up even before they finish recording their thoughts.

A journal can also be like a trash can where you empty the garbage from your mind onto the blank page and close the cover. Keeping a journal isn't likely to be the miracle cure for your depression, but it can be another potent resource to strengthen your mental health.

TRY THIS . . .

Using a spiral notebook, or whatever you have handy, jot down your thoughts and feelings about recent events that have impacted your life. Remember, you're writing only for yourself, so say anything you like. Start out trying to write at least a few sentences every day. Later you may find that a different schedule is more to your liking. Although frequent writing is not a requirement of journaling, it usually provides the greatest benefit. But don't let *not* writing cause you any guilt at all!

28

MEASURE PROGRESS

— From My Journal —

Another note from Anita

Dick,

Good morning! I know you were up reading very late last night so I doubt if I'll see you before I go. You remember, I promised Aunt Grace that I would help her with her shopping today. I don't expect to be back until around dinnertime, but I left you some of last night's stew for lunch. It's on the second shelf of the fridge.

I can tell you're a little down these last few days but from a longer perspective (since January), it seems to me your depression has improved a lot. I find it impressive the way you're able to work on yourself when you slip down. I often find those little slips of paper with affirmations written on them in your pockets (in fact, I've recycled a couple for myself). I've watched you drag yourself off the couch to work on the new brick walk in the perennial garden; it's really looking great. Where you find the strength, I can't imagine. Sometimes you start off a little grumpy, but more and more you seem to be able to break through depression's snare to find your old enthusiasm again. You remind me of little Stacey. She skins her knees and bumps her nose but she keeps going and going and going—so do you. She's not about to give up and neither is her Grandpa.

I can say for sure, you have more heart than anyone I know. Defeat? You don't even know the word. Depression chose the wrong guy when it picked on you.

Love,

Anita

THINGS TO CONSIDER

One perplexing aspect of depression is that you often have trouble telling whether your mood problems are getting better or worse. After a woeful week, you may feel you've been detoured back to the agonizing place where your troubles began. But have you? If you look more realistically at your progress over a longer period of time, you'd likely find you've made great strides in understanding and treating your mood illness. Certainly improvement never seems to come fast enough to anyone plagued by depression.

One solution for lifting your mood is to deliberately measure your progress so you can better understand how you're doing. You can do this in several ways, such as reading past journal pages or actually making a list that compares your good and bad events of recent months. Sometimes it helps to ask your therapist or a trusted friend to help you make a realistic evaluation of how you're doing. Another advantage of doing an evaluation is that you can change or add new therapies if you find your improvement has not kept pace with your expectations. Borrowing the spin tactic of the politicians can show you how to put a more positive face on the events of your day while ignoring the less favorable aspects. This doesn't mean you can turn a terrible day into a great one. It does mean you can learn to minimize trouble by viewing it realistically and finding some good in almost any situation.

TRY THIS . . .

Whenever you feel you're not making progress solving your depression, take the time to evaluate your progress to date. You can do this from memory, but with difficulty. A better way is to review your journal notes and compare one period to another. Remember that even small successes are important because together they can add up to victory.

29

SOLUTION

SAVE ONLY BEAUTIFUL PICTURES

— From My Journal —

S ometimes I should just 'fess up. I was a real bear at the office this morning, growling at everyone in sight. My depression makes me feel like I'm losing my grip on things, and that I need to show I'm still in control. By lunchtime, I knew I had to get out of there. Arriving home, I headed for the old grape arbor in the far corner of the yard, rather than inflict my bad mood on Anita. The arbor is in rough shape. "Not worth repairing," I tell myself. The book I carried with me offered a subtle message that I wanted to be left alone.

I eased myself down on the worn wood bench and, after a while, my racing mind slowly shifted into idle to calm my anguished mood. My why me? resentment began to fade as my eyes were drawn to the gnarled old apple tree growing on the knoll above the ravine. Through the magic of memory I was transported back to my boyhood home in southern Ohio.

It's autumn back home, and I find myself on the top rung of a ladder which leans against my neighbor's apple tree. The tree hangs red with apples, and Mr. Barrows is steadying the ladder and telling me *what a good climber I am. I'm nine, maybe ten, and I feel important as I stretch to reach the choicest fruit at the very top of the tree. My pay is all the apples I can eat and a basketful to take home to Mom.*

The neighbor's barking dog soon jarred me back to reality, but those few minutes of enchanting memory provided a healing respite that pushed depression down a few notches on my worry list. I headed to the tool shed to get a paint scraper, mumbling as I went, "Maybe the old arbor is worth preserving."

THINGS TO CONSIDER

Life can sometimes lure you down an inviting pathway that terminates in a thorny bramble, or leave you stranded like a sailboat on a calm sea. One thing you can be sure of is that life will provide you with some trying times. But in between these difficulties will be promising sunrises, the joy of good books, coffee with a friend, and the laughter of children. You shouldn't be surprised to find life a mixture of good and bad; it's always been that way.

One interesting thing about life is that it lets you choose which moments to capture as memories. Picture each essential event of your day as a photo opportunity. Then decide which photos you will save for the memory album of your mind. Will you snap the traffic cop who gave you a ticket on your way to work, or will you keep the picture of your smiling daughter as she bolts through the doorway after school? The choice is yours.

When you open your photo album on some future day, will you find it full of fond remembrances, or will the pages contain mostly scenes of pain and difficulty? Yesterday's memories become the cornerstone on which you build today. Save only your best.

TRY THIS . . .

Using a very brief description, list the essential events of your day—both good and bad. Then circle the happenings you chose to save in your "memory photo album" and cross out the rest. Did you save the right ones? Practice this exercise often, until you learn to save only your good memories. The mere act of thinking about them is a mood-lifter.

PERFECTION IS NOT PERFECT

— From My Journal —

W hy do I find myself magnifying tiny flaws into catastrophic problems?

I've always believed that perfection was a worthy goal, but lately I've begun to realize that trying to fix every flaw only drives me deeper into the doldrums of depression. Chasing perfection offers failure as its sure reward. I want to pursue a new goal of just doing the best I can. What difference does it make if I finish first or last, as long as I'm happy with my effort?

This little discussion I'm having with myself today about perfection reminds me of the second or third visit to my psychiatrist. Dr. Leighton seemed to be probing for the cause of my frustration that day, and one of his questions caught me off guard.

"Tell me about your spouse," he said, "What is she like, and what do you think of her?"

I hesitated, wanting to be honest and not wanting to sound negative. Finally, I said, "She's not perfect—but when I compare her to the wives of all of my friends, I wouldn't trade her for any of them."

I'm striving to change my thinking so that my aspirations match the real world instead of some utopia that doesn't exist. If only I could learn to see a panorama of life in which flaws blend invisibly into the fabric! I know I'm not there, yet, but this effort has already brought a little more joy to many of my days. It doesn't take a mathematician to add up the plus and minus columns of my life and know that gratitude should be my result.

THINGS TO CONSIDER

A perfect place, a perfect friend, a perfect job—you hear people everywhere talking about a perfect something or other. The problem is that striving for perfection is much like searching for that pot of gold at the end of the rainbow: Ain't no such thing. If you use perfection as the standard for your life, expect disappointment to follow. It's an unattainable goal and the person you will most likely disappoint will be yourself.

How well you do something doesn't necessarily determine your level of satisfaction. Trying something new, even if the results are marginal, often provides greater rewards than continuing to hone a skill you've already mastered. Mistakes provide learning opportunities that teach important truths and offer exciting discoveries. Happiness comes not from concentrating on things you do perfectly, but from doing things that bring you delight. Changing your focus about perfection won't be easy, but the rewards of a happier life make it worth the effort.

TRY THIS . . .

First make a list of three situations where you've been disappointed because something you tried was less than perfect.

Then list three things you've never done but would love to try if no one (including yourself) was judging you.

CREATE SOMETHING

— FROM MY JOURNAL —

*F*or several months now, I've had this idea of building a rocking horse for my grandson Jacob, and today I finally decided to tackle the project. Surprisingly, as I refined my rough sketches, the rocking horse I first planned turned into a rocking-race car. "This will thrill him," I thought.

Next, I made a quick trip to the building supply store to pick up some lumber and other materials I needed. I began by laying my pattern out on the wood, tracing it and then cutting out the parts. As I worked, I kept thinking, "That boy is going to love this race car!" (The truth was I loved making it.)

When Anita called me to lunch, I was too busy to stop, so I grabbed my sandwich and headed back to the garage. Sanding is a tedious chore but I wanted the racer to look really good, so I carefully smoothed out every imperfection. Assembly is where the real fun begins—seeing the rocking-race car take shape. "It looks good," I repeated to myself as I reminisced about my younger days, when I built birdhouses, bookends, and all sorts of stuff.

At last it was ready for paint, the part I like best; bright red with yellow wheels, trimmed in black. I thought it turned out beautiful. The only thing left to do was add the name "Jacob" in bold letters on the hood, but that would have to wait until the base paint was dry. "He's going to love it," I kept saying over and over to myself.

As I write this story in my journal tonight, I'm amazed at the way this project awakened my creativity and totally captured my enthusiasm. Depression never stood a chance against that little red race car.

Things to Consider

Everyone can create. Children call it "making something." Obviously painting, sculpting, and writing poetry are creative endeavors, but so are a million other things, like building a dog house, baking a cake, tending a garden, or redecorating a room. Most of us have at least one project tucked away somewhere in our minds. This dream often stays hidden because we are afraid—afraid others won't appreciate it or may even ridicule our effort. Perhaps now is a good time to revisit that creative urge and give it a try.

There are a couple of important concerns you should consider before you begin. First, decide whom your project is intended to please. If it's you, then make sure that you alone are the final judge, and be prepared to disregard any negative comments.

Second, start with a project that you can handle without excessive frustration. "Making something" can stimulate your mind with positive thought and feed your soul with confidence and self-esteem. Creating is an antidote for depression.

TRY THIS . . .

Make a list of three creative projects that are within your skill and means. (Don't worry about being overly ambitious. No one's judging, and in a way, the smaller the better.) Then choose the one that you're most passionate about. Select a time and place to begin and lose yourself in creativity.

32

DO IT ANYWAY

— FROM MY JOURNAL —

Fear is harassing me once again tonight. Anita left more than an hour ago and I am terrified to be home alone. I can find no reasonable origin for this beast that rips my psyche to shreds. I managed to put up a good front when Anita left, but just watching her car disappear down the road filled me with panic.

For almost an hour I have paced back and forth in front of the window, sneaking a look at the clock out of the corner of my eye as if it might ridicule my cowardliness. I pick up the newspaper and try to read, but not a word of it registers in my head. I'm desperate. I try to pray but there's no connection.

Continuing to pace the floor, I finally wander out to my workbench in the garage and rub my hand over the rough edges of the new bookcase, which I haven't worked on for weeks. Grabbing a piece of sandpaper, I began to smooth the wood. Waves of panic and fear fight to claim control of my thoughts but I keep sanding. I'm scared and angry about what's happening to me.

Almost two hours later, I hear Anita's car in the driveway. She's *home! She asks about my evening but I act nonchalant, revealing none of my fear and panic. I'm trapped between wanting to confide in her, and hating to look like a wimp. I feel like a torn kite, flung about the sky and trying not to crash. God, how I wish I could find the peace I used to know.*

THINGS TO CONSIDER

Overwhelming fear and crippling apprehension can infiltrate your mind and harass you like a schoolyard bully. You hesitate to tackle even mundane tasks; maybe you even imagine sinister discussions going on behind your back. These common burdens of depression can send you spiraling downward.

Depressive fear freezes you with indecision and then chastises you for being unable to choose. A simple decision such as, *Should I attend a certain family or social event?* often creates a dilemma that leaves you too distraught to decide. Then, when you finally choose, depression will immediately try to convince you that your choice is wrong.

So, if you're going to be chastised regardless of your decision, why not go to the wedding or family reunion and be involved? At first, your heart may pound and you could feel short of breath and ill at ease, but *most likely* you'll end up having a good time. More important, every time you face your fear and *do it anyway,* another crack appears in the wall of depression; the more cracks, the more quickly the wall collapses.

TRY THIS . . .

Prepare several small reminders such as bookmarks, sticky notes, and mini-posters with the words, "Do It Anyway!" in bold print. Place these where you will see them often, as a reminder not to give in to fear.

P.S. If you think there will be too many unwanted questions from others who see your written reminders, then abbreviate the words to DIA.

33
SOLUTION

POSTPONE WORRY

For months I've listened to the coal train rumbling down the tracks, headed to Somerset Power Plant. It roars by about two in the morning, and it's usually trailing sixty or more cars heaped with coal. Many nights I've tossed from side to side, unable to sleep while the train's shrill whistle pierces the night's silence at every little crossroad. It's not that I don't love trains, but this routine has become such a constant reminder that worry has gotten the best of me again and I'm unable to get to sleep. This nightly battle is difficult to describe but, like the coal cars, worry just keeps rumbling through my head, offering one false premise after another. A few of these may contain some fraction of truth, but the vast majority are generated by the voice of doom that twists reality into dreary fabrications and churns my stomach into knots. Deeper and deeper I sink into the worry that feeds another sleepless night.

It isn't that I haven't tried to break this debilitating worry habit. I have. I've tried disputing the accuracy of these vicious lies, ridiculing them, pushing them out of my head with poetry, and getting up to read or snack. Sometimes these things help a little, but too often the lies seem stuck to my brain and nothing I try will dislodge them.

Recently though, I've discovered a little trickery of my own to drive this deceit from my mind. It's surprisingly simple and easy to do. My tactic is to no longer even try to challenge these perverse predictions but instead I tell myself that I'll just set aside these problems for now and worry about them tomorrow. When tomorrow comes, these vicious lies most often dissipate as the light of day reveals how ridiculous they really are. Occasionally a problem does remain, but the clear thinking of my morning mind makes it much easier to resolve.

THINGS TO CONSIDER

There is nothing underhanded about using a few tricks to outwit depression. One of the best tricks that humankind ever invented was procrastination. For most people, especially those of us with depression, it's a terrible trick we play on ourselves. But why not use procrastination *against* depression? Your mantra? "Worry about it tomorrow."

Try other tricks, too, things like switching to your scrapbook project when you feel your spirits starting to dip, taking a walk to relieve the boredom that's trying to trap you in your chair, or promising yourself to do something small to get you started on that bigger project you've been neglecting. Ideas like these could be labeled tricks but if they help to minimize depression, why not use them?

Since a good night's sleep is a great aid to restoring our energy and equilibrium, it doesn't hurt to use a trick or two here also. A glass of warm milk before bedtime works for some people. A half hour of reading or watching TV works for others. And because *worry* often overruns your mind at bedtime, remember to procrastinate. Worry tomorrow, sleep tonight.

TRY THIS . . .

The next time depression starts troubling your sleep with words of woe and threats of dire consequences, don't even try to challenge it or eliminate it. Instead use the tactic of postponement. Do this by writing the problem on a pad of paper by your bed and telling yourself that you'll figure out the solution tomorrow. When tomorrow comes, you're most likely to find that your mountain of worry has shrunk to a molehill.

34 SOLUTION

LOOK GOOD—FEEL GOOD!

— FROM MY JOURNAL —

mom *always preached to us kids that "Clothes don't make a person." Thinking back now, I realize that she was hoping to make us feel better about wearing the hand-me-downs of our siblings. My trial with depression has taught me that Mom's statement about clothes wasn't entirely true:* looking good does have a significant bearing on *feeling good.*

I stumbled downstairs today in my pajamas, thinking I would go back up and get dressed after I had my coffee. Instead, I spent the morning moping around the house, looking like a tramp and feeling sorry for myself. I probably would have stayed that way all day, except for the call from my brother, Ernie. Actually, I didn't take the call myself, or I would have told him to stay home. Anita answered the phone and told Ernie it would be fine for him to return today the grill that he had borrowed last week for the Little League picnic.

"Rats!" I roused myself off the couch and headed up the stairs. "Why does he have to come today?"

As I glanced in the bathroom mirror, it was obvious that my appearance was a disaster. I pulled myself into the shower still muttering, this time about the water being too cold, although when I got it adjusted, it felt awfully good. Then I pulled some clean clothes out of the drawer and got dressed. The whole process took maybe a total of twenty or thirty minutes. Standing in front of the mirror again to comb my hair, I could see a rather miraculous transformation. But more miraculous was my change of attitude. I actually felt better!

My brother dropped off the grill half an hour later and hurried on to other errands but I felt better the rest of the day. Look good—Feel good: It works.

Things to Consider

There's definitely a correlation between looking good and feeling good. Surprisingly, even when you're alone, looking good helps prevent the "loser" mentality that often creeps into your depressed psyche to rob your energy.

Lethargy sustains depression. If you're still sitting around at noon, looking like a mess in a ragamuffin robe, it becomes difficult to find the motivation to do anything positive. Your negative mind voices will offer many excuses: "Getting dressed takes too much effort," "Who cares what I look like anyway?" "I don't have the energy to fix myself up right now."

Summoning enough willpower to accomplish even a small

task can be difficult during encounters with depression, but one way to achieve this is by using the *one small step* approach. Begin by agreeing only that you will get out of bed or out of the chair that you have been sitting in for too long. Then you commit to a shower or bath. Next, you summon enough energy to shave or apply a little makeup and conclude by getting dressed. Learning to look good is another solution that helps move you toward recovery.

TRY THIS . . .

The next time you find yourself lacking the motivation to look attractive, go to the mirror and ask yourself if this is the person you want to be. Then consent to taking *one small step* to improve your appearance. This small step will make you feel better about yourself and may provide the momentum to accomplish more.

35
SOLUTION

USE ANYTHING THAT WORKS

I had my regular appointment with Dr. Leighton today, and some-how our discussion got stalled on the biological malfunctioning of the brain. He talked about serotonin, norepinephrine, neuro-transmitters, electrical impulses, etc. That stuff just confuses me. I'm not much into medical jargon but I did understand that depres-sion causes some sort of a chemical imbalance in our brains—or maybe it's the chemical imbalance that causes the depression. It doesn't matter as far as I'm concerned. Getting rid of this curse is all I care about.

The doctor's discussion reminded me of my teenage conversations with my father, who was an auto mechanic. Dad often felt it neces-sary to explain to me the principles of the internal combustion engine, but the truth was I didn't much care. All I wanted was to get my old car running so I could go out cruising on Friday night.

My guess is that Dr. Leighton's purpose for our little technical talk was to prepare me for a change of antidepressant medication. If so, that was unnecessary because to me it's not much different from *my family doctor, who tried several blood pressure medications before finding the right combination to treat my high blood pressure problem. Same thing as far as I can see.*

What I really learned today is that solving depression often requires multiple solutions. Medication, therapy, and a strong self-help effort seem to be the best approach—at least for me. Truth is, there's not much I wouldn't try to eliminate this torment.

THINGS TO CONSIDER

Recently, a friend revealed to me that he'd refused the depression medication recommended by his doctor. He was fearful of becoming dependent on it for the rest of his life. The facts are that when drug therapy is prescribed for depression, it doesn't always require long-term use. But if longer-term use is needed, why would it be such a big deal? Many people use medication indefinitely for solving dozens of different medical problems. So if a small pill can help restore your clear thinking, why not use it? Of course, you should never try new medications or change your current dosage without the guidance of a qualified professional.

Keep in mind, also, that you are not limited to one therapy. You can use various depression-fighting approaches at the same time. Most self-help solutions in this book can be done on your own unless you prefer to consult with your therapist first. Your commitment to stay with new medications or therapies is essential because they often require a period of adjustment before providing the desired benefits.

The phrase, "Use anything that works," should be firmly planted in your mind and posted where you will see it often. Your willingness to try any solution that seems reasonable can speed your recovery.

TRY THIS . . .

Write *Use anything that works* inside the cover of your journal or calendar. Then prepare a list of every new idea that you would consider using to improve your depression. Then choose one of these and try it. Continue your search by adding new therapy ideas to your list and eliminating the ones that don't seem right for you. Always consult a mental health professional if you are unsure whether the solution is right for you.

HOLD ON

— From My Journal —

Another note from Anita

Dick,

You keep talking about what you "have done to me," like you've injured me in some way. It's true that depression has restricted our family travels, and maybe we don't do quite as much as we used to but, honestly, we're doing just fine. For as long as it takes: That's how long I'll stand by you because my love for you means a lot more to me than cute cards and silly gifts.

Besides, I can still see your smiling face when I woke up from the anesthetic after my gallbladder operation a couple of years ago. I couldn't chase you from my bedside. And even after I got home, wasn't that you who went to the corner store after midnight to satisfy my craving for pecan ice cream? Now it's my turn to help you. . . . Isn't that what marriage is all about?

Dick, I know your recovery seems way too slow, but I can sense optimism filtering back into your life. I'm sure one day all this pain will be left behind us, and we'll be stronger for the struggle. I'm hoping I never find myself ensnarled in such agonizing woe, but if I do, you've left a road map of courage for me to follow.

Love,
Anita

THINGS TO CONSIDER

To those who have never been there, it's difficult to explain how devastating it is to realize that depression's shadows are once again drifting in to darken your world. The blues sneak in so silently that you're almost always caught by surprise. And even though you try to tell yourself it's not happening, you instinctively know that depression has somehow tripped you up again.

Depression is the damper that dashes your hopes and tries to push you back into a corner of despair and isolation. Yet in spite of this debilitating distress, you have to conjure up the strength to reach deep inside yourself and find the needed resources to cope with this unseen enemy. Even if you've prepared yourself for such occasions, fighting back is tough, and if you haven't prepared yourself, it can seem impossible.

What anchor do you reach for to get you through such adverse times? Some people call it persistence, others determination.

You may see it as plain old stubbornness that refuses to give in. Regardless of what you choose to call it, this resoluteness is the essential quality that carries you through the tough times. It is the power that lets you crawl back into life's ring to fight another round. Depression necessitates persistence because it is a struggle that consists of multiple rounds. Only when it finally becomes clear that you're not quitting will depression begin to slink away.

TRY THIS . . .

Prepare yourself for the next sneaky attack of depression by making journal notes about such occasions in your past. Review your many depression-fighting tools and prepare to use them the next time this illness tries to entrap you. Finally, renew your promise that you will never stop searching until you find the road that leads to your recovery.

37

SOLUTION

SHAPE UP

— FROM MY JOURNAL —

my trek this evening across Hopkins Meadow and around the high school athletic field was pure delight. The path had a light covering of snow and, as I reached the edge of the baseball diamond, there stood a beautiful doe with two spotted fawns chewing on the few remaining leaves of a beech tree. We stared at each other for a couple of minutes until they danced off into the thicket like a ballet troupe.

As I was heading back toward home, the sky was striking, mostly deep purple, but I don't know if that means good or bad weather for tomorrow. What I do know is that the panorama of a beautiful sunset always seems to connect my soul to a world of splendor. I love the big picture it provides, in which I can see my depression not as a conquering illness, but as a glitch of life that can be overcome.

It was just a little over two months ago that I left my safe, cozy couch and began my evening walks. At the beginning, I promised myself that I would try walking for at least a week, but now I'd never give it up. On occasions when I've skipped my walks, either *because of other obligations or adverse weather, I've usually felt lethargic the next day. My treadmill is still there and I suppose I'll have to switch to it when the weather gets really nasty, but it won't be nearly as much fun. Walking has helped me shed a few pounds and improve my mood. I have high hopes that this stint of melancholy will soon be over—this time for good—but I suspect that I'll keep walking as long as I live. There are just too many benefits to give it up.*

THINGS TO CONSIDER

There are many therapies for reducing depression, and exercise is one of the most important. If you're not already involved with regular exercise, you should consider its proven benefits. You may think of exercise as a way to get in better physical shape, but studies have demonstrated that it can also be an effective mood booster. There are thousands of ways to exercise, which range from mild to strenuous. Think of exercise as anything that gets you out of your chair and moving your feet. In fact, some types of exercise can even be done while seated. Factors such as your age, health, and condition are important in selecting an activity. If you have concerns about whether a certain type of exercise is right for you, it may be best to consult with your doctor or therapist before beginning. Exercise is usually the primary purpose of activities like walking, swimming, or aerobics, but exercise can also be the secondary result of other things like gardening, photography, hunting, or shopping. Start slowly with your exercise program because setting the bar too high at the beginning can discourage you before you've given it a fair test. Few things will pay greater health dividends than exercise.

TRY THIS . . .

Decide on an exercise plan that feels right for you, and put your plan in writing so you can refer to it often. It may be a walk around your block each evening or an hour working in your garden three times a week. Perhaps you want to use a treadmill or join a health club. Start slowly and make a serious commitment to keep going for at least two weeks, because it takes time to get into the routine and feel the benefits that exercise offers.

SKIP THE PITY PARTY

— From My Journal —

Youthful memories of growing up on our little Ohio farm often slip into my consciousness in spite of all the intervening years. Remembering how our pigs loved to wallow in swampy mud holes until they were caked with dirt from head to twisted tail reminds me of the way I sometimes slosh around in self-pity. I never understood why wallowing in mud felt so good to a pig, and I sure don't understand why wallowing in self-pity appeals to me.

Yesterday Anita suggested we go out to lunch and then visit the art show at the Community Center. I was slumped in my chair sifting through my mind for something or someone to blame for my depression. I was intent on feeling sorry for myself. Anita coaxed me several times to go with her. I liked the attention of her coaxing and sympathy, so I kept stalling, certain she wouldn't go without me, that is, until I heard her car pull out of the driveway. Then my anger flared: I can't believe she left without me!

I sat there sulking for a couple of hours more before I smartened up enough to realize that I was the only person feeling sorry for me.

I managed to drag myself out of the chair, grab a few bites of leftover pizza, and head out for a bicycle ride. I knew I needed to do something. As I shifted through the gears on my bike, my brain began to change gears, too. I thought about the way this episode of self-pity had backfired on me. Sloshing around in mud holes may be great for pigs, but when am I going to learn that my mud-hole tricks to win sympathy don't work very well for me?

THINGS TO CONSIDER

Self-pity is an enticing trap that promises relief from the harsh blows of depression. You feel misunderstood and confused about the plight of your illness. You can't understand why you have been singled out, and you want someone to acknowledge that you got a raw deal. This is the mind state where self-pity and sympathy-seeking can seem appealing. Maybe you've already used your illness as a crutch to achieve a more sympathetic response from other people. For example, you want to watch the football game on TV instead of visiting your elderly Aunt Ethel, so you tell your spouse you're not feeling well; maybe you'd better stay home. Maybe you feign fatigue because you don't feel like doing your exercise routine, or you don't want to go to work or school today. Seeking sympathy from others and feeling sorry for yourself has tempting benefits, but using them could be compared to using illegal drugs to gain temporary euphoria. It's a descending stairway that leads to deeper despondency and greater isolation.

TRY THIS . . .

Think about situations where you have used self-pity or attempted to solicit sympathy from others. Write in your journal about the futility of these actions, and think about ways to eliminate this self-destructive behavior. Promise yourself that you will guard against the future use of self-pity and find more constructive ways to demonstrate and *eliminate* your low spirits.

39
SOLUTION

BUILD BRIDGES, NOT WALLS

my old footbridge, which spans the ravine between the backyard and the woods, finally collapsed with the spring flooding. I wasn't surprised; I've been patching it up for years. Last weekend I started work on a new bridge made of pressure-treated lumber that has a nice arch to it and curves a little toward the west. Putting in the support posts and building the framework wasn't much fun because I had to wear rubber boots and stand in the mucky water. Today is better because I'm nailing on the deck, and with every plank I'm getting closer to the other side. I marvel not only about how good it looks, but that I'll soon be able to walk back and forth between the yard and the woods again without wading through the muck. That's important because this little half-acre woodland means a lot to me. It's where I go to get away from the din of life, my shelter when the storms of depression try to knock me down. That rough wooden bench is one of the few places where I'm able to restore my distorted perspectives and get back in sync with the world.

As I nailed down the final boards, one by one, I was reminded that

adding planks to a bridge is a lot like fixing depression. Every suc-
cessful therapy adds another plank, and one of these days I'll be
over that long bridge of depression, too, and fully connected to life
again. I'm getting closer and closer.

THINGS TO CONSIDER

A bridge connects you to a place that you could not otherwise go. A wall isolates and confines, shutting something out or keeping something inside.

Compare the actions of your life to a bridge that transports you across the swamp of depression and reconnects you to the fullness of life that you desire. Your bridge will require strong planks such as friendship, exercise, music, humor, prayer, gratitude, service, etc., to carry you to that depression-free destination. And every bridge requires maintenance to prevent the rot of self-pity, distortion, and doubt from wearing away the underpinnings that provide stability and support. Keeping your bridge strong may require medication, therapy, and the assistance of others. If you need help, accept it graciously, because one of life's lessons is that by *working together* we can accomplish so much more.

Understand that the storms of life will inevitably provide setbacks that damage the bridge you've worked so hard to build.

When this happens, your best response is to begin making repairs immediately. Don't switch your effort to building walls of isolation and loneliness that will restrict your life.

Success rarely comes from constant forward motion but is more often achieved by people who never give up. A wall or a bridge: Which will you build?

TRY THIS . . .

Take a page of your journal or notebook and draw a vertical line down the center. On the left side, list all the good planks, such as friends, music, laughter, gardening, etc., that make your recovery bridge strong. Then, on the right side, list the problems that tend to damage your bridge. Study all the items on your page carefully and think about ways to add more good planks and ways to begin eliminating the problems.

40
SOLUTION

NEVER GIVE UP!

— FROM MY JOURNAL —

T his is the hardest thing I have ever done—fighting depression. Day by day I struggle on, hoping this dark veil will soon be lifted so joy can flow back into my life, yet nothing changes. There's no bounce left in my step or in my heart. I feel useless, like I need to apologize for being alive. The deepest hurt comes from feeling like I've let down the people I care about the most. Not long ago I thought I'd left this depression ogre behind me, and now I find myself back in the same hole of doubt and desolation. How many times must this vicious cycle of hope and despair play out?

This is the first time in a week that I've attempted to write in my journal, and I can feel the venom spewing out of me. I tell myself that I must write; it's therapeutic . . . that I have to smile and hide my pain . . . that I have to keep searching for the truth that will set me free. But I'm tired—tired of trying to pull myself up again and again. I'm tired of looking for hope when everything appears hopeless.

Perhaps even scarier is where I may be headed. Where I could end up? These are the questions that wake me in the night and shadow me with melancholy. I used to be a person of reason and common sense, but I can find nothing about this wretched illness that makes any sense. My muddled moods roll in like storm clouds from nowhere to wash away the few faint rays of hope that still remain, and here and there the sun breaks out and tricks me into thinking that it'll stay. It never does.

What I would give to be my old self again and find once more the happiness I used to own!

Things to Consider

You can count on days when depression will paint a dark and dismal picture of everything related to your life. You may feel like the doors of hope have been slammed shut: You're devastated. At a time like this, where do you find even a flicker of hope?

You have to begin by questioning the validity of such feelings. Are things really as bad as your mind is telling you? Chances are that the desolation you feel has little to do with reality and a lot to do with depression's despicable trickery. This ploy of hopelessness is the ruse depression uses, not just on you, but on every person fighting this battle. This is the time to seek the truth by talking with a friend or counselor. This is the time to listen to your favorite music, write in your journal, watch your favorite movie or TV show, or just get up and *move*—anything that calms your fears and refutes depression's lies.

It helps to prepare in advance for such days in order to take as much of the punch as possible out of depression's torment. Learn to clearly identify the culprit as depression instead of some other malady (or "your own fault") and have your plan ready to cope with such difficult days. If everything else fails, simply *hold on*, knowing the dark clouds will eventually begin to drift away so that you can find the help you need.

TRY THIS . . .

Read about depression, talk with others, and try to understand all the ramifications of the illness you're fighting. Make notes of how a depressive episode begins: What are the signs of its onset? Its departure? What can you do when the next bout hits you? Knowing what to expect and being prepared helps lessen the anguish of a downcast day. Expect tough times, but remind yourself often that you're tougher than this illness.

41
SOLUTION

STAY INVOLVED

I spent all day dreading the dinner party Anita planned for tonight. I know I agreed to it, but that was several weeks ago, on one of my better days. Tonight I wasn't up to entertaining anyone. I never was much good at small talk and besides, in my current state, I can't imagine anyone enjoying my company.

I purposely came home early, hoping I still had time to convince Anita to postpone this party business, but the minute I walked in the door it was easy to see that I was too late. The table was already set with the good china, the house was straightened up, and I could smell something baking in the oven.

When Rod and Sally arrived, I smiled and put up a good front. They're rather laid-back folks and if they detected my sour mood, they didn't let on, although the conversation did feel a bit strained and awkward at first. Partway through the meal, the talk switched to politics and the conversation was soon punctuated with raised voices of jabbing humor as everyone kept trying to talk at once. It was a jovial mood around the table and I found myself caught up in the fun.

When Rod and Sally left a little after eleven, I was reluctant to see them go.

Looking back at the evening allows me to better understand how staying involved is important in overcoming the isolation and lethargy that too often consume my days. Tonight was a lesson about staying connected to life.

Things to Consider

There is no nice way to say that depression is a liar, but anyone who has experienced this ordeal knows it's true. This illness plants preposterous lies in your head like, *"Your job is in jeopardy,"* *"Your friends have forsaken you,"* *"You're looking old,"* *"You're no fun anymore,"* and *"You're a loser."* These outrageous accusations seem unending and they're devastating enough to make you want to slump onto the nearest couch and withdraw from life. *Don't!* Even when your mind is screaming, *"I can't! I'm too tired, I'll make a fool of myself,"* don't back out of life. It's not always easy to stay involved, but nothing about the depression is easy. Each time you rally your courage and deliberately engage yourself in activities with family, friends, and others, you become a stronger person. And don't be surprised to find that when you do participate, your apprehension most often fades away and you end up having a great time.

TRY THIS . . .

Make a list of situations where you've opted out of a particular opportunity but later regretted it. Think about how you can remain more involved in the future, and make notes about several specific places where you're planning to engage in hobbies, recreational activities, and social events. Follow up on your plan to participate, and don't let depression make you back down.

42
SOLUTION

HEAL OLD WOUNDS

— From My Journal —

Walking down memory lane can be enjoyable, but sometimes it can be counterproductive, to say the least. The latter happens most often when I search through old childhood memories, looking for clues of my depression. It's a rather futile search that dredges for faults and bad times instead of focusing on the wonder of my youth.

There is no denying that my father was an alcoholic who was often without a job, and that this contributed greatly to the insecurity of our family. And my mother's heart problems, which she often used as a threat to make us behave, made the future always feel tentative for me. Somehow I was the one who shouldered the most guilt for Mom's bad heart. I remember one upsetting occasion when I raced upstairs and hid in the attic, although my crime was nothing more than a childish squabble with my brother. I can recall the horror of thinking I had somehow injured my mother's heart. I crouched there in the corner of the attic, making a pact with God to spare my mom until I was grown up. In return, I promised to behave myself and mind my parents. Although I reneged many times on my end of that deal, God kept his promise and spared Mom until I was twenty-three.

Looking back to my childhood, it's not hard to see where guilt, fear, and anxiety first surfaced in my life. Those times were tough for our family financially, and in many other ways. I'm not sure exactly how these youthful problems connect to my current depression, but I suspect they do. More important is that I learn to shelve these troubling memories, not stew on them, and focus instead on those glorious days of youth, which were many, in spite of our various difficulties. Rafting on Sickle's pond, building tree forts in the old orchard, and riding bareback on our old mare Jenny—these were but a few of the priceless times I choose to remember.

Things to Consider

Some mental health professionals believe that adult depression may be rooted in childhood. A review of your youthful years can sometimes offer understanding and insight to help resolve this illness. Obviously, you can't change whatever happened to you in the past, but you can reexamine the validity of troubling grudges in a more charitable light.

As kids, when we used to make accusations and complaints about our siblings, my mother used to say, "People who live in glass houses shouldn't throw stones." It was her way of reminding us that we weren't perfect, either, and that our brothers and sister had their own accusations to fire right back at us.

Maybe you cling to unresolved issues as ammunition against someone. Or perhaps you harbor secret feelings that you are personally responsible for difficulties or disagreements in your family. Possibly you still bear the emptiness of feeling unloved by parents or siblings whose real problem was their own inadequacy rather than any animosity toward you.

If you have such unsettled issues from your past, this can be your opportunity to break the feelings of injustice that mar yesterday's wonderful memories. Compassionate understanding coupled with forgiveness can lift you to the higher ground of healing and happiness.

TRY THIS . . .

Find a quiet place where you can allow your mind to replay those haunting events of your childhood. Scribble notes about your feelings, write in your journal, and strive to understand the truth. Talk to those involved and make allowances for their imperfections. Wipe the slate clean with forgiveness so you can shelve these memories and live your life without the weighty baggage of past difficulties.

SPECIAL NOTE: If this exercise creates excessive pain and anger and upsets you, seek the help of a professional therapist to assist you in resolving such matters.

WORK ON YOURSELF

— FROM MY JOURNAL —

makeovers seem to be the big thing these days. Everyone wants restored youth and vibrancy. I'm guessing this means a lot of new business for the spas, gyms, plastic surgeons, and others. That's good for the economy.

I could use a little revamping, too, but I'm thinking more in terms of a mind makeover—sprucing up my mind with new positive viewpoints and erasing the doubt and bewilderment that have victimized me too long. I'd like to trade the skepticism of depression for a strong mind that has the "search capabilities" to find the good in almost every situation.

A mind makeover... Ridiculous? Maybe, but I can't think of a logical reason why not. Nothing but fear is stopping me from rearranging my thinking in bold new ways. I could begin with forgiveness—settle old grievances that distance me from family and friends. I could trash my quest for perfection and learn to accept life—flaws and all. Then I'd be ready to sign up at the health club and get myself in great physical shape to match my new mind. What *about dusting off a couple of those old dreams I'd given up on? I'd like to find that inquisitive kid again who lives somewhere in me, the one who sticks his nose into flowers, chases butterflies, and gets lost among the stars on a clear night.*

Just as I'm warming up to this mind makeover business, the doubt of depression begins to seep back in to remind me how silly this all is. Too late! Every transformation starts somewhere deep in the soul, and this one has already begun to take root.

THINGS TO CONSIDER

It's comforting to know that none of us is a finished product. Every day, for as long as we live, we keep evolving as individuals. You're neither the same person you used to be nor the person you will become in the future. The question is, do you want to participate in the process of shaping and molding the future you? Or, are you resigned to accepting the "*Que será, será*" outcome: "What will be, will be"?

By simply reading this book, you have acknowledged that depression is a problem in your life and that you are committed to taking an active role in resolving it. Searching out and implementing solutions requires work and perseverance. A resolute determination to *work on yourself* is the key factor to becoming a better you. It's not too late to reshape yourself into the person you want to be. It's not too late to begin your own "mind makeover."

TRY THIS . . .

> Using pages from your journal, describe the person you intend
> to become in the future. Then make a list of the changes that
> will be needed in your life to achieve this transformation.
> Finally, with the understanding that change requires both
> patience and perseverance, find at least one area in which you
> can begin to move in the direction of your dreams.

44
SOLUTION

ADOPT A PET

— From My Journal —

nancy has been in her room all day today. Her mother took her
up a tray, but she won't even come downstairs for meals. Our
popular teenage daughter seems to have totally rejected all help in her
time of crucial need. We've been to her door many times, and it never
opens more than a crack. No! She doesn't want to talk; she's fine—
just leave her alone. *Girlfriends stop in but no one stays for long—
no one except Amber, Nancy's gentle golden retriever. Even through
the crack in the door, I can see Amber lying there beside Nancy on the
bed, and sometimes through the closed door I can hear her muffled
voice talking to the dog. Her room is in total disarray, but all we care
about is lifting her out of this stupor so she can find a little hope to cling
to. Losing a boyfriend to suicide has devastated Nancy more than I can
begin to imagine, and where it will lead scares me even more.*

Our suggestions about the need for counseling have been totally
rejected. She's almost an adult, so we can't just rush in and drag her
out kicking and screaming. As parents, we feel so helpless and confused. I'm not sure our thinking is even rational anymore.

Added two weeks later:

Nancy's bedroom door has begun to open more often in the past week, and she has come out to face the world again. Nancy has always loved her dog, but now Amber rarely leaves her side. Often you see Nancy's hand slide down to smooth Amber's fur. Conversation has restarted and Nancy even talks a little about the days ahead. She's a strong person and in time will heal. The pain of this awful tragedy is enormous but there's a hero, too, a loving dog named Amber. Where would we all be without her?

THINGS TO CONSIDER

If we keep our hearts and minds open, life will often surprise us with unexpected help to heal our depression. For many people, that help comes in the form of a pet. It could be a stray dog that you adopt or a tiny kitten, like the one I found hiding under my back steps one day. Exactly what the animal is or how it gets to you makes little difference. The real question is the devotion and bonding that can happen between an animal and a human being.

The task of caring for an animal can give people reason for their existence. It's difficult to forsake an animal that repays you in love and devotion, and the hurt and anguish of a serious ailment become easier to bear when your pet nuzzles close and covers you with animal kisses.

Many studies have been done to determine the value of pets to speed healing and enhance well-being, and the results almost always show a conclusive benefit. Many animals seem to have an intuitive sense about the needs of their owners and are often credited with saving property and lives. A pet can add comfort in troubling times and add a loving dimension to your life.

TRY THIS . . .

If you like animals (and if you're able to take care of yourself, day to day), consider adopting a pet. The animal shelters are filled with pets looking for a good home who would love to be your companion. Their unconditional love and affection can help offset the trauma of a bad day. Providing for a pet can provide you with purpose and fulfillment in your life.

45
SOLUTION

SEE YOURSELF STRONG

— From My Journal —

I feel like I've been robbed, like someone stole my confidence and clear thinking. My true identity has somehow been swapped for that of a dejected person whom I don't even know.

Without a valid reason, I've lashed out at everyone in sight this week. I feel bad about my negative behavior, but most of all I regret the squandered potential of those wasted days. My only consolation is the certainty that this pathetic behavior has got to belong to someone else—it's certainly not me. I can't help wondering why I should have to battle just to hang on to my real self.

One thing's for sure, I didn't cause my own depression. So why do I constantly sense that it's my fault—that I've somehow screwed up my own life? On days when the veil is lifted, I can clearly see that my difficulties connect to depression, but even that provides little comfort. I know that somewhere beneath this despicable gloom, the real me is always waiting to return. I've got to ditch this deceitful illness that tilts my moods and find my way back to wholeness again. Whatever it takes, I'm ready to begin.

Tonight I'm flipping back through the pages of my mind to find those strong images of myself before this hell began. I need to hold on to those joyful times when I was happily engaged in life and able to handle its give and take in stride. That's the way I used to be, and that's the way I will be again.

Things to Consider

To say that you can *lose yourself* sounds silly, but that's exactly what happens with depression. You have trouble remembering the strong, upbeat person that you were before this illness began. You begin seeing yourself weak and struggling as this beast tries to corner you. It feels like depression has plagued you forever, and you wonder whether you'll ever be able to break free.

This is the type of thinking that obsesses a depressive mind, twisting the truth until surrender often seems like the only option you have left. These are the tough spots of this illness, when you need to crank up your courage and refuse to trade the *real* you for a *depressed* you.

Reinforcing your memories of the confident person hidden under depression's veil helps keep depression at bay. One of the ways to restore these strong images of your past is by digging out old photos, personal awards, mementos of your successes. These can serve to remind you of the strong, confident person you were in the past and offer assurance that you can be that person again. These positive images can become the motivation for staying on track as you work to restore a more positive outlook for your life.

TRY THIS . . .

Search through old photos of yourself taken before this illness began and find a few from your best times. (If you can't find any, no doubt your friends and family would be thrilled to oblige.) Enlarge these if necessary and display them as a collage, along with other mementos such as trophies, award certificates, cards, letters, diplomas, etc. Almost anything that you take great pride in will serve as a reminder of who you really are.

46
SOLUTION

COMPARED TO WHAT?

— FROM MY JOURNAL —

Anxiety and depression have a tendency to turn me inward as I search for reasons for my illness. Today I've been trying to remember my first episode, but that was a long time ago. I think I must have been around twenty-one or twenty-two, living alone for the first time, near Buffalo, New York. I began waking up in the middle of the night with chest pains, profuse sweating, and a pounding heart. At the time I didn't even know a doctor, but my friend Sam talked me into going to his.

I don't remember much about the visit except this little short doctor with a mustache walking into the examining room where I waited. He just stood there for a minute almost staring at me, then asked in a gruff voice, "What's your problem?" I told him about waking up at night with chest pains, the pounding heart, the whole story. He gave me a skeptical look, put his stethoscope to his ears, pulled up my T-shirt and listened for a minute or two while I took deep breaths.

Dropping the stethoscope from his ears, he again looked directly at me and said, "There's nothing wrong with you. Some people have a pain in their arm; some people have a pain in their back or their knee or their elbow. You have a pain in your chest—so what? Everybody's got a pain somewhere. You're fine."

That was the end of my visit, and remembering all this today I'm thinking, that guy sure wasn't much of a doctor, but he was right about one thing—almost everyone does have pain somewhere. And, as much as I hate it, I could probably have something even worse than depression.

Things to Consider

Depression often seems like the worst thing that could ever have happened to you, and undeniably it's a terrible illness filled with pain and difficulty. The self-pity that infiltrates the mind of most sufferers is a common reaction to this ordeal. It is almost impossible not to think about how unfair and unlucky you were to be snagged by this beast.

Yet from a larger viewpoint, almost everyone receives an ample share of heartache and misery of some type. In fact, if you randomly selected someone from the telephone directory and could closely examine his or her life, you would probably find serious episodes of pain and suffering, and even ill health. It's a part of living that very few people can escape.

To achieve a more accurate perspective of your own adversity, imagine for a moment that you were required to choose one serious affliction from the multitude of miseries that befall men and women. Which one would you choose? Cancer? Heart failure? Diabetes? A crippling auto accident? The loss of a family member? Or depression? Mental illness is never to be minimized, but you need to understand that there are situations worse than depression. Mood illnesses can be successfully treated and sometimes eliminated. That enough is reason to find optimism for your future.

TRY THIS . . .

Accept the fact that you have been afflicted with depression, but remind yourself that there are worse things to suffer. Then get to work, using every available means to improve and eliminate your mood problems. Strive to root out self-pity as if it were the plague.

47
SOLUTION

NO MORE FISH STORIES

— FROM MY JOURNAL —

What a fool I've been! I've wasted the past three weeks of my life, convinced that I had cancer. It's difficult to believe that I could reach this bogus conclusion with so little to substantiate it.

My PSA score had risen a few notches and my family doctor, in her usual take no chances approach, had asked me to see a urologist. "Nothing to worry about," I recall her saying.

Of course, I knew that the PSA test was to determine the likelihood of prostate cancer, and I wasn't even out of her office before I'd convinced myself that I was doomed. While I waited the three weeks for my appointment with the urologist, I spent practically all my spare time researching prostate cancer and speculating about how serious mine might be. I even reviewed the various treatments, thinking seriously about which one I might choose.

My visit with the urologist was last Tuesday, and today I got his call. I was expecting to hear the "C" word I'd been dreading for so long.

Instead he began with, "Everything looks good."

"Looks good?" I interrupted. "What about the cancer?"

"Negative—you have no cancer."

Instantly I knew that I had been duped. I remembered how miserable I'd made myself these past weeks, wasting countless hours in worry. . . . The agony of sleepless nights. . . . The fear that had me lashing out at everyone around me. I could see now that I had been a fool and I began to attack myself as I have so many times before. "You're an idiot! How could you have been stupid enough to think you had cancer?" *This time I knew the answer to that question—* depression!

THINGS TO CONSIDER

Depression tends to make you exaggerate your problems, much like the boy who went fishing and caught a small fish. Later, when he held out his hands to show his mother how big the fish was, he kept spreading them farther and farther apart.

Every day, almost without exception, some sort of crisis pops up, something breaks, something goes wrong. Difficulties are as much a part of life as the air you breathe. Usually you can understand and successfully deal with these setbacks. But when you allow depression to exaggerate the smallest obstacle into a catastrophic problem, a solution often seems impossible.

Exaggeration can twist even positive words of a friend or spouse into a personal rejection. It can turn a frown from your boss into, *"I'm losing my job."* People who suffer from depression should probably establish a rule that requires downsizing their problems by at least fifty percent to achieve any reasonable sense of accuracy.

Whatever method you choose to adjust your faulty perception, you should begin with the understanding that exaggeration is a normal part of depression and correcting this distortion leads to a healthy mind.

TRY THIS . . .

Make a list of three recent examples where you exaggerated a problem. As you list them, try to remember the details of each instance and the agony you would have been spared if you had challenged those faulty perceptions and adjusted them for greater accuracy. The next time you have a problem, use this exercise as a reminder to take a second look, to be sure your assessment of the situation is accurate.

LISTEN CAREFULLY

— FROM MY JOURNAL —

Yesterday I began complaining that the garbage truck showed up a day early, and of course I didn't have the trash out to the street. Anita promptly reminded me that she had read me the notice several days ago, and only yesterday had mentioned a second time that the town was altering the trash routes because of the upcoming holiday.

"I don't remember that," I said.

Her response was, "That's because you never listen."

That accusation is not exactly true because I do listen, at least part of the time. I always hear her call to dinner, and I never miss an invitation to visit a used bookstore. Lately, though, I have begun to realize that my hearing seems more attuned to bad news than the good stuff.

When I offered a suggestion at the church board meeting Tuesday night, Joe Elshelman said, "I don't like Dick's idea because we lack the personnel to carry it out." Well, the only part I heard was, "I don't like Dick's idea," and my blood began to boil. In fact, I'm told Joe went on to praise my basic idea, but the truth is that I was too busy stewing to hear the rest of what he said.

My brother recently teased me about my big gut, and although I pretended to laugh and jab back, I later found myself looking in the mirror to see if I really was gaining weight. These days I seem to be able to pull a negative word or two out of a conversation and miss every good thing that is said. Psychologically my hearing has gotten a little screwed up by depression. Maybe they make a hearing aid to restore accuracy?

Things to Consider

Accurate hearing is rarer than you might think—for almost all of us. You've heard the expression, "Don't believe everything you hear." But on some occasions, we hear things that were never said. Healthy minds tend to filter out most of the unimportant, negative stuff rather than perseverate on it. This helps maintain a positive mood. Depression does the opposite.

As a young boy, I had my mouth washed out with soap a time or two for saying things that were not true. My mother had little tolerance for lying. Yet depression's lies make it difficult for those of us who suffer this illness to accurately register what our ears are hearing. Our lowered confidence and poor self-esteem act as magnets to collect any negative phrases and exaggerate them beyond recognition. The depressive mind turns smiles into smirks and whispers into suspected indictments of everything we do. Our faulty hearing can even turn our friends into enemies if we construe their well-intended words the wrong way.

Sorting out the truth from what you hear, rather than accepting depression's twisted version, is essential to restoring good moods. Depression fades as truth is clarified.

TRY THIS . . .

Consider recent situations in which you may have heard someone's remarks differently than they intended. Now think about adding a mental ten-second delay that enables you to make sure your interpretation is accurate the first time. Wouldn't this "truth filter" eliminate a lot of grief?

49

ACCENTUATE THE POSITIVE

— FROM MY JOURNAL —

Depression slips in and out of my life like a sly fox. Today that fox is harassing me again, so I'm fighting back with a trick of my own. I'm leafing back through my old journals but only reading the pages that contain good news. I'm skipping the places that talk about dark times, much like I skip the stock market report on those days when the Dow takes a big tumble. I need no reminding of how bad things can get.

Leafing through my old journals, I find many places where I wrote about important breakthroughs in my fight with depression. They begin with the page where I first admitted I had depression, after denying it for so long. And I wrote a lot about the day when I finally cranked up enough courage to visit a psychiatrist (how I had resisted that meeting!). Then there was the day I finally understood that, in spite of all the depression-fighting resources available, the responsibility for getting rid of this villain belongs to me. I think the most important writing I found wasn't even part of a journal page. It was a pledge I scribbled in the margin that I would never accept depression as a permanent part of my life, no matter how hard the fight or how long it might take to defeat it. I had no way of knowing then the tough times that lay ahead.

I found one unmistakable truth that stood out clearly on all the pages I read today: Winning every battle is not nearly as important as never giving up.

Things to Consider

Have you ever seen anyone with his or her head twisted completely backward? Of course not, but that's what it feels like when depression turns your thinking from a positive to a negative focus. And even though common sense keeps telling you that this reversed viewpoint is wrong, depression has a way of outsmarting your good logic.

Winning the depression battle requires you to concentrate on the positive things that are happening in your life. Tactics like meditation, self-talk, and affirmations help to do this. Another effective strategy is to actually write down your accomplishments and then review your list often. Seeing your achievements written on paper makes a bolder impression in your mind.

Bedtime reflection of the day's achievements not only provides a better night's sleep; it also helps you wake up the next day in a more upbeat mood. Focusing on good things brings more good things: It's as simple as that. Healing depression is a slow process, but every small step in the right direction moves you closer to victory. Remember those steps!

TRY THIS . . .

> Find a small notebook and label it "Victory Book." In this book, record only positive aspects of your life, such as steps forward in your battle with depression, other accomplishments, good fortune you've experienced, and anything else that makes you a winner. State your strengths and successes boldly, without concern for boasting or redundancy. Keep this "Victory Book" handy and refer to it often as proof that you're a winner.

50
SOLUTION

STOP BLAMING YOURSELF

— From My Journal —

Another note from Anita

Dick,

I can't help but notice that you've been heaping a lot of blame on yourself lately. You seem to think that everything that doesn't work out exactly right is somehow your fault. You were talking about our diminished social life last night and speculating that it's because no one wants to be around you in your downcast mood. Actually, I think the problem is that the kids have been in so many activities in recent weeks that we simply don't have time or energy left to entertain much. But when we do go out with friends, you always seem to hold your own and we usually have a great time. You talk also about how you have neglected things around the house, the broken porch rail, the weeds in the garden, the peeling paint on the house. Well, as far as I'm concerned, if you add them all together they don't amount to a hill of beans. Nothing we can't catch up on when we get a little more time. Maybe I shouldn't say this, but aren't you a bit like

Chicken Little, trying to hold up the sky all by yourself? Could it be you're listening too closely to that depression voice again?

As far as I'm concerned, what really counts is the significant progress you've made these past few months controlling your moods. For certain, you are more outgoing and more involved than before. Let the paint peel and the weeds grow. I don't plan to lose any sleep over it. What I care about is you.... You and me and the kids—that's what really matters to me.

Love,
Anita

THINGS TO CONSIDER

One of depression's worst traits is the tendency to make you feel responsible for everything that goes wrong. The world around you seems to rest fully on your shoulders. Your mind tries to twist and magnify every problem into a catastrophe that has your name written on it. You're to blame for everything, and everything includes depression itself! How many times have you felt that there must be some flaw or weakness in your thinking that allowed depression to invade your life in the first place? It's not unusual for sufferers to question whether there is some defect in their character that allowed this deplorable illness to take root.

Yet when people have difficulties with caved-in heart valves, misshaped corneas, and crippling arthritis, they don't consider themselves responsible for their defective body parts. Your brain is a body part, too—in fact, the most complex and arguably the most susceptible of all. For some reason, when it malfunctions, depression sufferers conclude that they must be at fault for their illness. This is typical of depression sufferers' distorted thought process, and eliminating it leads to the reduction or elimination of your mood problems.

TRY THIS . . .

> I remember the time my sixth-grade teacher caught me chewing gum in class. She made me write: *I WILL NOT CHEW GUM IN CLASS*, five hundred times on the blackboard. Maybe depression sufferers should use a few pages of their journals to scribble, *I AM NOT RESPONSIBLE FOR MY OWN DEPRESSION*. This is a lesson you have to learn and retain in order to purge this illness from your life.

KNOW THE POWER OF WORDS

— FROM MY JOURNAL —

I would have bet that affirmations wouldn't work. Too simplistic, almost silly, was my take on the whole idea. What could be the value of repeating the same few words over and over again? Of course I'd never used an affirmation in my life, but that didn't stop me from having an opinion. Then depression nailed me, and I began to search for ways to correct the situation. I guess I was pretty desperate the day I came across that old book *The Game of Life* written back in the 1920s by Florence Scovel Shinn. Otherwise I would have never decided to try affirmations. Shinn explained the how and why of affirmations, offering one on almost every page of her book. By this time in the course of my depression, I was willing to try almost anything, and I figured I didn't have much to lose by trying a couple of these. That must have been about a month ago and —Wow!—the results have been amazing beyond anything I would have believed.

The affirmation I started with was I'm on the road to recovery, and then I added Look for the good things today and Thank You, thank You, thank You as reminders to be more appreciative of all the

blessings I do have. *Affirmations seem to infiltrate my mind help-
fully, helping to keep it focused on positive outcomes. Like everything
else, there's always a catch. To benefit from an affirmation, I find that
I must deeply believe the premise, keep it simple, and repeat it often.
I suspect there are a million theories about why affirmations work,
but the why doesn't interest me much. They work! So I plan to keep
using them.*

Things to Consider

Words have power. They can either send your spirits soaring
or plunge you into despair. Most amazing is the way a few well-
chosen words, repeated often, can change your life by changing
your thinking. These words of declaration are known as affirmations, and for many people they become effective weapons
against depression. To succeed, the affirmation should be short,
positive, and paint a strong word picture of what you want to
accomplish. Your own thoughts usually work best, even if the
prose is weak, although a quote or phrase written by someone
else can also work if you strongly accept the assertion as your
own. Simplicity rather than cleverness is the key. To work best,
the affirmation must be deeply embedded in your mind so you
can repeat it often, even under stress. The more indelibly you're
able to plant an affirmation in your mind, the more likely it is to

be realized. Below are two more examples of affirmations to aid a depression sufferer.

- This is no big deal! *(used for any problem that depression tries to exaggerate)*
- I won't let depression isolate me.

Try This . . .

Write at least one affirmation. Post it in several conspicuous places where you will see it often during your day. Repeat it at least twenty times each day for at least a week. Then decide for yourself whether affirmations work for you.

52

SOLUTION

SEEK POSITIVE PERSPECTIVES

— From My Journal —

Holidays have a way of deflating me. I'm not sure why, except they never seem to live up to their stellar billing. It's Christmastime again and, most of all, I'm disappointed in myself. I had all those great gift ideas, but I've procrastinated so long that no one can expect anything unique from me. My big plans to decorate the front of the house aren't going to happen, either. I've waited too long, so why bother now?

My mood was pretty low tonight, with depression dragging me down and the holidays making me feel like I didn't count for much. That's when something almost miraculous happened to change my outlook. I was slouched there in my chair, half watching the TV; again this year they were playing that old movie It's A Wonderful Life. Like everyone else, I've watched this thing a dozen times or more over the years, but there was one part tonight that really caught my attention. It's the part where George is up in heaven looking down on his hometown, lamenting that he had failed in his efforts to help the folks. Then he slowly realizes (or maybe the angel shows him) the

154

great good that resulted from his small deeds and many acts of kind-
ness. George was amazed to see how his life on earth had accom-
plished such far-reaching consequences.

That's when I got to thinking about my own life and the people I've
helped. Sometimes my gifts were quite substantial, but more often
they were small: a word of encouragement, a good reference, a co-
signature, a smile, or a few bucks. I'm thinking now that when you
tally up my good deeds, maybe I haven't done so badly, either.

Things to Consider

Depression makes you lose an accurate perspective of who you
are and turns you into your own worst enemy. Criticism always
hurts, no matter who delivers it, but the mental beating you
inflict upon yourself has no equal. The voice in your head that
dishes out these false and damaging lies is the root of the illness
you suffer. To correct depression, you must find a way to uncover
the truth and correct the pervasive lies that try to infiltrate every
crevice of your heart and mind. Allowing this deception to prevail reduces your opinion of yourself until you begin to question
your own value.

The solution begins by clarifying who you are, what you stand
for, and the good that you have accomplished. It is vital that you
review this truth often and develop as many ways as possible to

dispute the voices that portray you and your accomplishments in a false and negative light.

TRY THIS . . .

Take your journal or a notebook and begin writing down every person you can think of whom you've helped over the years. This help may have been only a kind word, a note of encouragement, a little gift of some kind, or assistance with a problem; or it may have been something much larger. Anything you've ever done that's made even a small difference in someone's life, counts. Then elaborate in a positive manner on the difference your assistance *may* have made in these lives. Don't be surprised if you get tired of writing names or your memory fails as the list of people you've helped grows much longer than you expected. This is the simple proof that you have touched many lives in significant ways and made a difference more profound than you can even imagine.

53
SOLUTION

FIX A BROKEN DAY

— From My Journal —

Today was one of those calamitous days when everything seemed to go wrong. It started this morning with me locking the keys in my car at the convenience store. I finally got to the office and had hardly set my briefcase down when I was confronted with an irate phone call about a billing mix-up. The afternoon didn't go much better.

Finally this evening, hoping to redeem a bad luck day, I suggested to Anita that we have dinner at one of our favorite restaurants on the other side of town. As we pulled into the restaurant parking lot, the sign "CLOSED WEDNESDAYS" stared at us. The words, "Trouble always comes in bunches," flashed into my mind and, regardless of how illogical that old adage may be, this day seemed to fit it perfectly. I shut off the car and leaned my head back against the seat, bewildered.

In the past I have often brooded myself into a deep state of despondency on days like this. I was at that point tonight until I began to see the ridiculousness of it all. Undeniably, it had been a day filled with minor screwups but lumped together, what did they really amount to? Was I willing to let depression sneak up on me again, all because of a few silly screwups?

We started back home, taking the long route around the lake, and stopped at the harbor just in time to catch the sun setting over the water. It was breathtaking! The little outdoor café at the marina was nothing gourmet but the burgers tasted great and the view was even better. We lingered over coffee, talking for almost two hours. It's been too long since Anita and I have connected like that.

Things to Consider

It makes no difference who you are: There will be days when everything just seems to fall apart. Trouble blindsides you, leaving no opportunity to brace yourself against the pain. Still, although you probably can't avoid troublesome days entirely, you can choose how you will respond to such trying times.

Begin by thinking of difficult days more like a bad roll of the dice, rather than some cruel force singling you out. Remind yourself that such days happen to everyone. You can choose to feel abused and sorry for yourself, or you can push aside the difficulties and search your memory for the positive aspects of the day.

Turning around a tough day starts when you adjust your perspective to a more accurate view of the day's events. Eliminate the negative exaggeration and stop thinking that it was all your fault. Balance the scales of a bad day by deliberately offsetting problems with activities that you enjoy doing. You have the power to soften the impact of a bad day, and sometimes you can even turn it into a triumph. Reversing a bad day begins by believing that you can.

Try This . . .

Using the thoughts above, consider various ways to help salvage your next bad day. Make a list of your best ideas and prepare to use them the next time the *Bad Day Blues* visit you.

54
SOLUTION

FIND YOUR SPECIAL PLACE

— FROM MY JOURNAL —

I purposely stayed up late tonight, hoping that once I hit the bed I could get right to sleep. It didn't work. For hours I twisted in the covers, wide awake. I tried repeating nursery rhymes, counting my blessings, and transporting my mind to exotic places. Nothing helped.

My mind kept spewing out dire predictions that my emotional problems were about to destroy me physically. I've been so tired in recent days that I can hardly drag myself around. My stomach and digestive tract are so messed up I might as well be buying my medications by the case. Sleep is the one thing that helps to restore me, but I've been robbed of that again tonight.

The clock on my nightstand kept reminding me of my predicament as I looked over and read two-thirty in the morning—I hadn't slept at all. I threw the covers off several times, trying to get up, but it felt like I was anchored to the bed. I finally managed to push myself off the side and drag my body down here to the one sanctuary where I can always find comfort: my easy chair on the back porch. It sounds crazy, even to me, but this chair has become such a good friend. It's

hard to describe the relief of sinking into its deep cushions and know-
ing that I won't be chided about my faults or accused of not trying to
help myself. I would never admit it to anyone but I'm in love *with*
this old chair.

THINGS TO CONSIDER

Slip away to some quiet place where you can leave behind the agony of depression. This could be a tree stump deep in the woods or a chair by your bedroom window. Any tranquil place will work, but keep in mind: A hopeful attitude will be the most important thing you bring.

You may choose to use your special place for meditation. If you've never meditated, you might want to give it a try. Actually, meditation is easy to learn, and numerous studies have shown that it can help to clear the mind of negative debris and offer fresh insights about your life. You may have heard about using crystals, secret mantras, and incense, but none of these are required. You can simply focus on your breathing, stare at an object, or recite a word to reach a state of bliss. There are many excellent books and articles to help you achieve success with meditation.

Other people use their special place to read aloud, pray (itself a form of directed meditation), visit with a friend, or write in their journal. A special place can become a refuge that allows you to see depression not as a catastrophe to be endured forever, but as a temporary illness that can be resolved with time and effort.

TRY THIS . . .

Look for a quiet nook that you can call your own, a place where you can be alone if you choose, a place where you can read, think, or write in your journal. If necessary, rearrange the furniture and find a comfortable chair. Do whatever you need to do to make the spot just right for you.

EXPECT SMALL MIRACLES

— FROM MY JOURNAL —

*L*ast Tuesday, Anita and I buried Amber, our golden retriever, beneath the lilac trees in the corner of the yard. I built a nice box from heavy plywood and we wrapped her in a beautiful quilt. Saying goodbye to that old dog was one of the hardest things I've ever done. I always believed she was sent from heaven to shepherd our daughter Nancy through the turbulence of her teens. Our family learned a lot about love and loyalty from that gentle dog.

Depression has been nipping at my heels again these past few weeks, and this devastating event had the power to set off a full-blown episode. Then the most amazing thing happened yesterday as I was dragging myself up the back steps. I thought I heard the cry of a kitten. I stopped and listened: Meow-Meow—it was a kitten. I couldn't see it but I knew it had to be somewhere under the stairs.

I called Anita outside and we both began trying to coax it out. Then we tried some milk and tuna, even hamburger, and got not even a glimpse of it. Reluctantly we left the food and went in for the night. This morning we tried coaxing it out again; no luck. That's when I *decided on more desperate measures. Using my crowbar, I pried off the top step and there it was: a tiny white ball curled in the corner, no bigger than a handful of snow.*

Afterward, I wondered what to make of all this. In the past I might not have thought much about this event, but lately I'm learning to find miracles in everyday events. Today, this tiny kitten switched our viewpoint from sadness back to joy again; that's a miracle to me. "Magic." That's what we'll name the kitten.

THINGS TO CONSIDER

One of life's most intriguing lessons is that it gives you about what you expect. Visualize good things happening in your life and that's most likely what you'll get. If you're anticipating trouble, you're sure to find it. For example, if you're headed for a party and you expect it to be great fun, it probably will be. Conversely, if you think it's going to be dull and boring, count on that. This same rule applies to lots of other things in life, like your finances, job promotions, personal relationships, and many more. You'll usually get about what you expect.

Are you expecting miracles to occasionally surprise you with joy? That's more likely to happen if your mind is open to such possibilities. You become like a magnet that attracts good from many places. You may have thought of these miracles as good luck, answered prayers, or good old serendipity. It doesn't matter what you call them as long as you recognize that your own positive expectations contribute to good outcomes.

A word of warning: You may think this sounds easy. *Expect good things—Get good things.* That *is* how it works, but beware. Depression will try to rob you of these positive expectations. You can stop this by challenging bad thoughts, reading uplifting books, listening to inspiring music, and doing dozens of other mind-enriching things. Teaching yourself to expect good things opens your soul to the wonders of life.

TRY THIS . . .

Prepare yourself to receive more small miracles in your life by making a list of three specific things you plan to do to instill greater hope and promise in your thinking. Friends, music, books, poetry, and prayer are but a few of the available resources for you to draw your list from. Many of these have something in common: Getting up and getting out. That's important, too. And don't be afraid to try something new.

YOU'RE IN GOOD COMPANY

— From My Journal —

I'm tired of hiding! I know the stigma of depression can be brutal, but I believe I'm now strong enough to stand up to it. A few narrow-minded people will always choose not to understand, but I'm no longer going to shoulder their prejudice as my problem.

Yesterday for the first time, I spoke publicly to a small circle of people at church about my illness. My hope was that it might save someone else some of the agony that I've endured. Jim Moore was sitting beside me and I could see the shock registering on his face as I told my story.

In fact, he hardly let me finish before he said, "Dick, I've worked with you in this church for almost twenty years, and you've never acted depressed."

His comments brought to mind my own family doctor, who for many years treated me for baffling bouts of exhaustion that left me so spent that I could hardly function. She was a wonderful doctor and tried every possible remedy, even referring me to several other medical specialists. Somehow depression was never identified as my problem.

Thinking now of the people I have known who have become tangled in this dark web brings to mind the myriad different and baffling symptoms each has endured. The many faces of depression can be difficult to recognize, and the stigma of shame and rejection keeps our masks tightly in place. I can never promise that my depression is gone forever, but I can say with certainty, "There's no more hiding for me." I've finally ripped down the GUILTY sign that depression had posted in my mind for so long. I'm ready to face life again—proud of who I am.

THINGS TO CONSIDER

The list of people who have achieved great success despite their depression is long: Ty Cobb, Charles Schultz, Virginia Woolf, and Vincent Van Gogh are but a few. The same goes for William Styron and Mike Wallace, both outspoken sufferers of depression. Abraham Lincoln, Calvin Coolidge, Winston Churchill, and Boris Yeltsin are among the world's great leaders who have suffered such melancholy. And American first ladies have not been exempt, either: Betty Ford and Barbara Bush have both talked candidly about coping with serious bouts of the blues. But don't be fooled into thinking this illness belongs to the famous, because the majority of sufferers are ordinary people who come from every walk of life.

In recent years, a more open dialogue has developed and many people—famous and not so famous—have come forward to talk and write with great candor about their depressive trials. This openness has helped to reduce the stigma that often binds people caught in this illness. Statistics vary, but most studies show that roughly one person in five will experience an episode of depression serious enough to need professional help at some time in his or her life. The good news is that effective treatment is available and the vast majority who suffer this illness can fully recover.

TRY THIS . . .

Admitting your depression to others can be a giant step toward liberating yourself. Your admission not only helps others to better understand what depression is about, but it can also increase your own confidence. Choosing the right time to do this is something only you can decide. Hearing of your depression, most people will be understanding and helpful, but you should also prepare yourself for the possibility that someone, usually because of ignorance, might make crude or inappropriate remarks or behave differently toward you.

57
SOLUTION

DO WHAT YOU HAVE TO DO

— From My Journal —

moving our Christmas tree has become a big joke around here. It's at least seven feet tall, and we moved it for the third time in a week. On Monday we switched it to the north side of the room, and this morning we had to clear the living room for the hardwood floor refinishers. The problem is that it's now in the middle of the dining room and that doesn't leave us any place to sit down and eat.

I remember how low I was the day we had to vacate our big farm home in September because of the fire. We were all devastated about leaving. We knew then it would take months to make the place fit to live in again, but we felt fortunate it hadn't burned down completely. Actually, we wouldn't be living back here now except the kids begged to come home before Christmas. At first Anita and I said, "No way." But after continued coaxing, we finally relented, with the understanding that there would be a lot of disruption and everyone would have to pitch in and do whatever needed to be done. So the trim work, electrical repairs, painting, and papering continue while we live in a state of chaos that accommodates the schedule of the work-men. I'm thankful the upstairs is almost finished so we can get away when things get too hectic down here.

In some ways it's been kind of fun, with the kids helping to sweep up the sawdust, paint the walls, and of course move the Christmas tree. Occasionally there is a complaint from the kids, or sometimes their mother and I just remind them that we all have to do what we've got to do if we want the house ready for Christmas. In fact that's sort of become the motto around here. Yesterday Jeff and Nancy were doing the dishes, and I heard him using it on his little sister. "Do what you've got to do," he reminded her when she complained about putting the dishes away.

Things to Consider

I wish someone had sat me down right at the beginning and told me the truth about depression, what to prepare myself for and what to expect. How was I to know that:

- Solving my depressive moods would be the toughest thing I had ever done.
- I should prepare to fight the biggest thief and liar of all.
- There were lots of resources to help me but the responsibility for solving my depression would belong to me.

🍃 Finding the strength and discipline to do what I need to do would be the key to taking back the control of my own mind.

Slumping in an easy chair is so much easier than doing what you need to do. It is so much easier to withdraw into yourself than to reach out to family, friends, and therapists. Knowing whom to trust and then trusting your family, friends, and mental health professionals enough to follow their advice and suggestions requires tremendous courage. Waiting for medication or therapies to effectively kick in requires both faith and patience. Hardest of all, sometimes, is trusting yourself enough to decipher the truth when your own mind is lying to you. It's courage far beyond the norm. Anyone who speaks of a depression sufferer as weak or cowardly should be pitied for his or her ignorance.

TRY THIS . . .

Take a page of your journal and write about your understanding of the effort it will take to triumph over your depression. Plant the words "I will do what I have to do" plainly in your mind as a reminder that there will be many things you would rather not do, but that you will do them anyway if that is what it takes to restore your good moods and clear thinking.

LITTLE THINGS MEAN A LOT

— FROM MY JOURNAL —

"*Little Things Mean a Lot.*" I've always loved that popular song from my youth, even though I've never given much thought to the validity of its message. Today's events taught me that little things can make a big difference in my mood.

It's Saturday and I was up early making plans to get a few things done around the house. The weather was a little brisk, but sunny, and I was busy preparing a list of chores as I sat down on the back porch with my coffee and began flipping through the TV channels. "Nothing on as usual," I thought, hesitating momentarily on a talk show program on which white supremacists were spouting outrageous statements of racial superiority. I watched with surprise at first, as they kept spilling out their rancor, and soon I became aggravated by their repulsive opinions. I continued watching a few more minutes before clicking it off in disgust and heading outside. Mowing was the first chore on my list, then repairing the handrail on the back deck. Through all of this I couldn't quite shake those hateful TV images or erase the troubling mood they had put me in.

After lunch I continued my chores until Anita called me to dinner, which gave me an excuse to put my tools away and head inside. Walking into the living room I found a card table set up with our good china and fancy linens right in front of the fireplace.

"Thought we'd have dinner here in front of the fire," she smiled.

We were halfway through our meal before I realized that this little candlelight dinner had sent my spirits soaring again. The words "Little Things Mean a Lot" drifted through my mind once more as I thought about the things that had propelled my mood in both directions today.

THINGS TO CONSIDER

You may think that solving depression requires major changes to have any real impact, but even small changes can contribute to a better mood. Everyone, but especially a person sensitized by depression, is influenced by the dozens of little events and occurrences in a typical day. Negative news from the television or newspaper can certainly alter your mood. Kind or harsh words from a friend or family member—even a stranger— can substantially affect how you feel. In fact, just the sight of a good friend has the power to reverse a bad day. Music, food, pets, weather . . . the list of things that can sway your mood is lengthy.

You have full or partial control over many of these mood triggers. If a certain photograph activates bad memories for you, get rid of it. If television news makes you feel negative, don't watch it. Restrict your books to those with happy endings if sad books put you in the dumps. Don't stay on the phone with people who upset you. You have a lot more influence than you may realize over the small daily events of your day, and *together* these events that often seem minor can have a major impact on your outlook.

TRY THIS . . .

Take a sheet of paper and divide it vertically. On one side, list all the small, typical events you can think of that enhance your day. On the other side, list those things that are downers for you. Keep adding to your list each day until you sharpen your understanding about these mood triggers. Use this information to begin eliminating and avoiding as many of the bad influences as possible and experiencing (and adding more!) good ones.

59
SOLUTION

TURN LEMONS INTO LEMONADE

— FROM MY JOURNAL —

Yesterday was one of those mixed-up days when the weather gods seemed intent on duking it out. I could hear the rain banging on the tin chimney above our bedroom, even before I was up. By mid-morning, the sky split open and the sun glared with such intensity that the yard felt like a sauna. The rest of the day was a duel between the rain and the sun until dinnertime, when the rain finally set in for good.

This scenario is pretty much how depression works for me. The sun (that's me) gives off its warm radiant glow, but the dark clouds (that's depression) drift in and hide the sun's warmth, much like depression hides the real me.

Standing at the rain-streaked window last night, I could feel the dismal evening getting to me. I knew I needed to do something or the doldrums of depression would soon overwhelm me again. In the kitchen, I could hear Anita starting dinner, so I'd need to move quickly with my plan. Trying to hide my anxiety, I walked up behind Anita and wrapped my arms around her waist. "How would you like to go out to dinner and a movie this evening?" I asked. She turned around to face me with an incredulous look, and then looked at the vegetables she had been cutting up on the counter.

"It's pouring rain out there . . ." she began. Then, without waiting for my answer, she broke away from me to start putting the food back in the refrigerator.

Reminiscing about last night, I can't remember when we last had such fun sloshing through the rain like a couple of kids. The evening destroyed all my theories about how dismal weather always escalates depression. Today I'm still basking in last night's victory.

THINGS TO CONSIDER

During the depths of your depression, it's difficult to find any redeeming value in this baffling illness. Yet in time you may realize that this woeful experience can provide valuable, life-changing lessons. Listing the benefits you've gained from this fight can reveal new pathways of personal growth and reinforce the progress of your recovery. Consider your newfound perseverance, won in the throes of misery by refusing to concede . . . your deep inner strength and clearer perspectives, both gained through difficulty, both making you a lot harder to trip up in the future . . . your lost arrogance and deeper humility, which leave you less critical of others and more charitable toward yourself. Depression's required lessons have the potential to provide a more satisfying life.

This illness has taught you how to manipulate the hairpin turns and swerve to miss the potholes scattered along your new pathway. The trials of depression have finally taught you that life is a mixture of good and bad and have prepared you for both. You now see your humanity as a strength, not a weakness—a strength that allows you to love and appreciate without requiring perfection.

TRY THIS . . .

Consider the beneficial lessons that depression has taught you, and focus on at least one. In your journal, write a little bit about the experiences that taught you this lesson or lessons. Note the benefits you have derived and how you will alter your thinking (and thus your life) to make it more satisfying.

BUILD YOUR SUPPORT GROUP

— FROM MY JOURNAL —

*I*f the devil chose me as a target for depression, then God must have selected my rescue team. It's a team that begins with Anita, who offers no syrupy sympathy, just solid support. I really appreciate the way she listens to my tales of lament and then helps me to find a ray of hope to ease my troubled thinking. She cheers me on like I was her knight in shining armor, always confident that the end of this adversity is near.

And Dr. Leighton—the guy's a prince. I must admit I began this journey scared to death of any psychiatrist, but now I see him as a friend whose quiet strength has been an immense help to me. I find it interesting how he's able to guide me down the right path without overt directions or criticisms. I've only had to call him a couple of times on an emergency basis, but it's always been comforting to know he's available day or night in case I really need him.

There are several people I depend on in my support group who don't even know they're team members. That's because I rarely mention the "D" word to Sally, Diane, or Bruce, yet they instinctively sense my down days and find ways to lift my spirits with their contagious joy.

Actually, until I read about it recently, I hadn't thought much about this "team" stuff. These people are all just friends to me, friends I can laugh with when I begin to take life too seriously, friends I can lean on when things start to get shaky. And when I fall, they're always there to help me up again.

THINGS TO CONSIDER

Depression is an illness that tends to push you toward isolation. The difficulty of this detachment is that it deepens the pain and hampers recovery. This is why a support group is needed to help you make treatment decisions and offer moral support to get you through the tough times. Almost every sufferer has some type of a support group. It may be only a spouse or a friend, but it might include a dozen or more people.

The front line of your support group will usually be family members and close friends. That's because these are the people you interact with on a frequent basis. Their supporting role requires patience, empathy, and honesty. Stay clear of those who badger, criticize, or patronize because these actions rarely lead to improvement.

An important part of your support group is often people with professional training, such as psychiatrists, psychologists, and therapists. Initially, you may feel apprehensive about seeing a professional, but after a couple of visits you will probably find they are both helpful and humane. Their responsibilities begin with a correct diagnosis, clear explanations, and recommendations for the best treatment options.

Your *confidence* is the essential element; no support group can be successful without it.

TRY THIS . . .

Think about and list the members of your "support group." How effective is it in helping you battle depression? Are there other people you would consider adding? If so, note this next to their names and begin considering ways to add them to your support team. Are there changes that need to be made to make your team more effective? Also ask yourself whether you are taking full advantage of your support group.

61

KNOW WHO YOU ARE

— From My Journal —

ANOTHER NOTE FROM ANITA

Dick,

I know you were quite upset yesterday with the thought that people were whispering about you behind your back. Frankly, I am not aware of any of this sort of thing but I would not be too surprised to find it true. We both know there are a few thoughtless, narrow-minded people who thrive on gossip. But as I think about it, I wonder what they might say about you. You have not, in recent months, made a secret of your depression, so that can't be hot news. Suffering from depression is not immoral or criminal—is it? Perhaps they say that depression proves you to be of weak character, but then how would they explain Lincoln and Churchill, who also suffered from this problem? All I can say is that if someone is blabbering nonsense, let's not bother bending down to hear it.

Now, on the other hand, I could whisper a lot of secrets about you.

No, not bedroom secrets; I'm talking about the way depression has strengthened you, made you more tenacious. You stand like an oak tree that becomes stronger by resisting the wind. You almost seem to mock depression these days with that staunch determination that brings you back to your feet every time you get tripped up. This is nothing to whisper about. No, I want to shout. You are a winner!... Winner!... Winner!

And I couldn't love you more,
Anita

THINGS TO CONSIDER

I can remember as clearly as if it were yesterday. I was a first grader, playing in the yard with several of my neighborhood friends, and Joey Dexter called me a "big sissy." I knew too well what "sissy" implied and, holding back the tears, I went racing into the house to find my mother.

"Mom, Joey called me a big sissy." Then I waited for her to stalk out into the yard and send Joey home.

Instead she asked me, "Are you a big sissy?"

"No! I'm not."

"Then calling you one can't make you one."

"But, Mom," I started to whine.

That's when she started to recite a little ditty that became famous in our family (and all around America, I later learned): "Sticks and stones can break your bones but names can never hurt you." She repeated it with me several more times until I had it down pat and went racing back to the yard with my new name-calling defense, which I came to use often (maybe too often) in the years that followed.

I later learned that while Mom's advice was good, her little ditty wasn't completely right—offensive names and unsavory remarks *can* hurt, sometimes a lot. And even good people occasionally say hurtful things. Yet the pain subsides quickly if we are secure enough to know who we really are.

Try This . . .

Mentally prepare yourself for the possibility of whispering and unkind remarks from people who are ill informed about depressive illness. Remind yourself that just because you have an illness, your worth and value as a person are not depreciated. It takes more strength and courage to fight this illness than the maker of any snide remarks will likely ever know or understand.

62

CELEBRATE EVERYTHING

— FROM MY JOURNAL —

I'm really thrilled about our first granddaughter, Stacey Ann. She has already become the princess of the clan. I was talking with her mother on the phone recently as she described the big celebration they're planning for her "one-month birthday": a cake with one candle, balloons, presents—the whole works. My first reaction was, "That's ridiculous, why would anyone have a big celebration for a baby that's only a month old?" The only thing sillier that I could think of was my neighbor who had a cook-out last summer to celebrate the blooming of her wisteria vine—first time in eight years, she claimed.

All this birthday commotion got me to thinking about what we should and should not be celebrating. The more I thought about it, the more apparent it became that maybe it was me who needed to adjust my own thinking. So many things worth celebrating are small things, like learning to ride a bike, seeing spring's first robin, or finishing the dining room curtains.

Anita surprised me in my den this morning. She carried in a tray with two freshly baked pineapple muffins and coffee, and said,

"We're celebrating my new riding lawn mower." Anita enjoys mowing the lawn and yesterday her new fancy-schmancy mower arrived. Sitting there in the den, she couldn't stop talking about the great features of her new lawn mower and how much she loves it. Not long ago I would have called her a little bit loony, but today I shared both her joy and the delicious muffins. Everybody around here seems to be celebrating something and maybe a little more festivity wouldn't hurt me, either.

THINGS TO CONSIDER

The secret of successful athletes is their ability to deliberately forget their setbacks and focus instead on the next opportunity for success. This sustains the positive attitude needed to triumph. This same philosophy applies to your battle with depression. You must learn to celebrate every victory, even the small ones, and erase your errors and setbacks as if they were words on a chalkboard.

Did you pull yourself out of bed and get dressed this morning? That's worth celebrating. Were you able to recognize the false message of doom playing in your head today and alert enough to switch channels? Write about it in your journal or tell a trusted friend. That little project you found too frustrating to finish last week—you completed it today? Celebrate! There's nothing wrong with directing a little well-deserved applause at yourself.

And while you're at it, why not celebrate your daughter's first steps, tonight's full moon, or a gorgeous day. Maybe dinner would be a good time to ask, "What are we celebrating today?"

TRY THIS . . .

Vertically divide a page in the back of your journal into two parts. On the left side list all the occasions you have recently celebrated, no matter how modestly, and on the right side write a few words about how you observed these celebrations. Look for such occasions and applaud every success in your life. Make celebrating a habit.

WHAT ARE YOU WAITING FOR?

— From My Journal —

Fixing my oatmeal this morning, I got to thinking about my difficulties with depression in recent weeks. It seems I solve one problem and two or three more pop up in its place. And my down moods haven't made me very popular with family or friends lately. It's sort of like running on my treadmill . . . going nowhere.

I've postponed a lot of things I've been wanting to do, afraid that depression will screw up any plans I make. But I'm getting tired of waiting for this curse to go away, tired of waiting for better times to come. Everything *feels like it's on hold* while I battle this bewildering ordeal. How long, I wonder? How long do I have to wait to find a little happiness for my life?

I have noticed that my friends and associates aren't exactly living in utopia either, even though their problems are different from mine. Problems and life . . . so often they seem to be tied together. What I find truly baffling is the lack of correlation between the severity of a person's difficulties and their ability to find happiness. Jane's mother is fighting ovarian cancer, yet she and Kevin are on their way *to Alaska. Jack is stuck in that wheelchair but he seems to have a great time coaching the kids in soccer. Am I missing something? Why am I sitting here on my duff, waiting until this depression business is over? Why can't I go out and grab a little joy along the way? Happiness and depression . . . sounds like such a strange combination, but I'm determined to try it.*

Things to Consider

You may think that your happiness is on hold until your depression woes are solved, but that's not necessarily so. Life is rarely all good or all bad, so the trick is to find as much joy as possible wherever and whenever you can. Don't wait for your mood problems to be untangled before you have a night out with the girls or head out to the ball park. Push depression aside (or go in spite of it) for an hour, a day, or however long it takes to do the things that bring you delight. Not only will these respites rekindle your joy, they will also keep the sun shining above the dreary cloud cover that depression tries to hang over you. And every time you push the clouds back, even for a little while, they become a bit easier to part. Push them back often enough and the clouds stay gone for good.

Quit waiting for the perfect time and situation. You need no excuse to restore a little happiness to your life. Maybe now's the time to start a new watercolor painting, bake that chocolate soufflé you've been wanting to try, or update that photo album. Depression never waits for you—so why are you waiting for it?

TRY THIS . . .

Start now to put more joy in your life. Make a list of pleasurable things you would like to do and start looking for opportunities to fit them into your life. And don't wait for the perfect opportunity—go when you get the chance and don't bother looking back to see if depression follows.

DON'T BE FOOLED

— FROM MY JOURNAL —

t was raining when I woke up—cold, gloomy, miserable. Around nine, I took my car over to the garage and, sure enough, they said it needed new brakes. That's well over two hundred bucks shot. I left the car and called Anita to pick me up. Sliding in beside her, I started right in on my litany of complaints: the lousy weather, the outrageous cost of the new brakes, the bank's screwup of our checking account. I didn't even like the haircut my barber gave me yesterday. On and on I droned until we reached the hardware store, where Anita wanted to pick up some curtain rods for the new bedroom curtains she's making. Waiting in the checkout line, I could hear an old farmer, several places in front of me, praising the rain.

"Wonderful rain!" he said, "slow and steady, just what we need. Hope it lasts all day."

"You're crazy," I thought, "praising this gloomy weather."

Driving home, those two words, "wonderful rain," stuck in my brain, playing over and over again. Rain does have benefits, I understand that. No rain, no crops—that's for sure. And since I like to eat,

I suppose that rain could be called wonderful, especially to a farmer. Slowly I began to realize the negative bias that had crept back into my thinking. Take the bad brakes on my car. Sure, fixing them would cost me some bucks, but that's a lot better than crashing into a tree or something worse. I mentally surveyed my list of gripes and actually found a positive side to almost every one of them. I could see now I'd been scammed again by the dreary spin depression puts on everything.

Things to Consider

Did you ever go to an amusement park funhouse with those crazy mirrors that can make you look as fat as a pig or as skinny as a pole? They have mirrors that will twist your face into a pretzel, and mirrors that will shrink your legs to your shoe tops. Depression uses mental flimflam in much the same way to convince you that your life is falling apart. It ridicules the way you look, the way you act, the way you work. It warns you not to risk anything because if you do, you're sure to fail. It tries to stick you with the blame for every bad thing that happens anywhere around you. Perhaps depression's most hideous fabrication is the lie that you're stuck with it forever and that it's futile to try to overcome it.

Depression is rarely a laughing matter, even when compared to hocus-pocus of a funhouse. The critical difference is that while you know the images reflected on the funhouse mirrors are just a ruse, you too often believe the false images that depression flashes into your mind. Only by teaching yourself to dispute depression's lies and find the real truth can you reclaim the rational thinking and sound judgment that rightfully belong to you.

Try This . . .

Draw a vertical line to divide a sheet of paper into two columns. In the left column, list several recent situations in which depression has tried to distort the truth and twist it toward the negative. Then use the right column to explain what the truth really was in each of these situations.

Repeat this exercise often as you learn to counter exaggerated, negative thoughts with the truth.

65
SOLUTION

THE TOUCH OF A HAND

I've been making great progress in my battle with depression for the last several months. In fact, recently I've been thinking that it might be over for good, but then Anita and I had a silly squabble about money, and I quickly found out that I still had more work to do before I could use the word "over" to describe my mood problems. That was a real disappointment that's left me moping around feeling sorry for myself for more than a week now.

Anita has been champing at the bit to drive out to Nancy's in Ohio, so I reluctantly consented to go; I'm feeling too burned out to get anything done around here anyway. Of course I can't help but smile when I see those three boys. It's interesting how little kids accept you as the person they know, instead of gauging how you might be feeling right then. Shortly after we arrived, we began playing board games and this ended in a free-for-all on the family room floor. Next they begged for me to take them to Imagica, the local book store (they know I'm a sucker for bookstores). So I loaded them in the van and off we went. Alex and Jake are old enough to use caution but

Colin is only four, so I made sure I had his hand as we walked through the parking lot toward the store. The thing I found amazing today was the way my troubles just evaporated when I was holding that precious hand. He clung tight, trusting me to lead the way. I was his comfort and his guide in a world that must look pretty big and complex to a small child. Soon we were inside the store and he wanted to be on his own, so I gave him some space and watched from a distance.

I've been thinking about that little episode. Sometimes my own world gets a little complex, and I could stand a little more hand-holding, too.

THINGS TO CONSIDER

Learning to reach out for a comforting hand in a time of need is not an indication of weakness but a display of strength. It takes a secure person to say, "Hold my hand, I'm a little down." Graciously, you can accept that comforting hand, knowing both of you will benefit. And you will be able to even the score by returning this supportive touch to others in the days ahead.

The source of that warm encouraging hand can come from a spouse, a friend, a child, sometimes a stranger, and often from God. You may think of God as being a long way off, but the length of His reach overcomes any distance, for those who believe. Whoever your source, this uplifting connection can only happen when you acknowledge your need and willingly accept the waiting hand.

Sometimes just a simple squeeze can provide the strength to get you through a tough situation. An arm to lean on can help you through a shaky time. A touch can change your life. This is not a crutch you use forever but a connection lasting only minutes, even moments, which provides the strength to see you through a rough spot.

TRY THIS . . .

Make a list of the people you know who would extend their hand to you in situations of need. (In addition to those your list, there are probably lots of others whom you can't think of right now.) Think about whether you're strong enough to reach out for help in your times of need. Realize that you'd almost surely be willing to provide that outstretched hand if someone needed your reassurance.

START WHERE YOU ARE

— FROM MY JOURNAL —

I'm in one of my contemplative moods today, as my depression slowly retracts and hope surges in to take its place. I've been thinking this evening about all of the influences that have shaped my life and made me the person that I am. Some of these influences I am very thankful for and others (like depression) I abhor.

I'm thankful for my good genes that have given me health, reasonable intelligence, and a tall physique. On the other hand, if I had a time machine I would have unchecked the boxes marked "alcoholic father," "grow up in poverty," and "dirty blond hair." And you can bet I would have unchecked the box marked "depression," too. Yet when I add up the whole package, it becomes obvious that life didn't shortchange me, even though I often act as if it did.

A thought has been flashing in my mind all day that says, "You take what you get," but I'm not so sure that's true. Some things I can actually change, such as the color of my hair, where I live, or my weight. On the other hand, it would be tough to alter my height or today's weather. My mind mulls this dilemma, trying to separate the changeable from the unchangeable, but that's not as easy as it sounds.

When I think about this in a broad sense, I realize that I do have the power to change almost anything by changing my perception of it. No one can change the weather, they say, but I can learn to love a rainy day. With the use of both reality and perception, I think I can change anything I choose to about my life.

THINGS TO CONSIDER

Everyone has certain aspects about his or her life that they would like to change. Some things like education, living conditions, and employment *can* be changed. Your height, your parents, and your place of birth are impossible to change. Grousing about the lot you've been given, or wasting your time wishing it were otherwise, only makes the situation worse.

One of the greatest discoveries of recent times is that people can actually reinvent themselves—but making meaningful changes is never easy. Since wishful thinking doesn't work, you must begin with the person you are and remold yourself into the person you want to become. This requires a clear understanding of the direction in which you desire to go, and a clear vision of the person you want to be. Taking those first steps is often traumatic, but there's no other way to begin. Detours and setbacks are normal as you attempt to make changes in yourself. Strong persistence is essential for success, just as it was in the fable of "The Tortoise and the Hare." Whether you make real changes in your life or change your perception of the unalterable, you have the power to become a new you.

Try This . . .

> Write down three negative things about your life that would be possible to change, and three more things that would be impossible to change. Reinventing your life requires that you have a clear understanding of which things are changeable and which are not. And remember—even if there's something or someone in your life that's unchangeable, you have the power to change your perspective on these.

67
SOLUTION

IMAGINE THAT

I've gotten myself involved in a real project these days. For weeks I've been out there in the woods, trying to turn a collection of discarded building materials into a little writer's cottage. I've got half a dozen neat old windows, a couple of oak doors thrown out by the school across the street, some rather beat-up light fixtures, and tons and tons of rough-hewn barn beams and weathered siding. Most of this stuff I've salvaged over the years from various yard sales, demolition sites, and trash heaps. I confess to loving all this old junk, but even more fun is trying to fit it all together to make myself the quaint little retreat that's pictured so vividly in my mind. Projects like these are nothing new for me; I've been doing weird stuff like this for as long as I can remember. I built my first fort when I was eight or nine, followed by several tree houses, a bicycle shop, and even a log house on a raft. An "overactive imagination" is what my mother called it, and I was never sure if that was a compliment or a complaint. I may have gotten shortchanged in my math skills and some other areas, but I have no trouble seeing things that don't exist.

With depression nipping again at my heels lately I'm beginning to understand that this vivid imagination of mine can be both a benefit and a curse. On one hand, my creativity keeps me involved in a lot of different projects and lifts my spirits. On the other, my "overactive imagination" sometimes hinders me by creating problems that don't exist. I can exaggerate molehills into mountains faster than anyone I know.

Things to Consider

Training your imagination to focus on the right things can be a real boon in solving your mood problems. You can do this in many ways: by writing, drawing, painting, gardening, cooking, and dozens of other activities. Anything you do that stretches your imagination makes you more capable of visualizing a better tomorrow. New ideas and new thinking let you see beyond today's difficulties to a place where hope and happiness wait. Imagination can open your mind up to try new therapies and fresh ideas that lift you out of yesterday's rut to higher ground, and encourage you to keep working to ease depression's drag. It's much harder to feel sorry for yourself when you're arranging flowers, burning a mix of your favorite songs on a CD, testing a cookie recipe, or designing a new bathroom.

There's one negative aspect of imagination that you must

guard against: Don't allow your mind to envision problems that don't exist. To correct this situation, you must learn to distinguish facts from fiction and refrain from exaggerating minor difficulties.

Imagination is a skill worth pursuing if you focus your creative mind in the right direction. Try to imagine your life without depression, then let your creativity help to devise ways to get you there.

TRY THIS . . .

Consider taking up a new creative activity to expand your imagination. How about trying to write a little poetry, or maybe scribbling down your memoirs? Drawing and painting can be fulfilling even if you're a beginner. There are lots of other possibilities, such as photography, decorating, sculpture, and wood-carving (I call it "whittling"). Because the mind has trouble thinking of two things at once, when you put your imagination to work, depression takes a backseat.

68
SOLUTION

CHOOSE THE RIGHT LENS

*T*oday started off with such a powerful promise of renewed hope. How I love springtime, when the seeds on our giant maple trees spin down like tiny helicopters and the forget-me-nots along the fence are a ribbon of lavender blue. Donna is back in the office today after being off almost five months with breast cancer. Having my secretary back is like having my right arm reattached. Things were humming and I can't remember when I felt so good.

One phone call from my brother-in-law was all it took to shatter my morning of elation. My sister, Martha, had been diagnosed with breast cancer. It was unreal, like some sinister plot. Donna's recovery had my mood soaring, but now Martha is victimized by the very same disease. Martha is so much more than just my older sister—she was my second mother. She fixed our lunch, dug the dirt from our ears, and kept my brothers and me from turning into heathens.

I shuddered with anguish. This was preposterous! What had she done to deserve this? I tried to pray but my words came out as rage. "Unfair! Unfair! Unfair!" I slammed my fist down so hard it hurt—

I could feel myself losing control. Dropping my head on the desk, my anger slowly drained away, replaced by a deep sense of emptiness. I'd been at this familiar crossroad enough times before to know which pathway to stay clear of, but was I strong enough to make the right choice? My sister was in trouble, and I could let depression take me down in grief and self-pity or I could reach out to help her.

I picked up the phone. We began with tears but ended in laughter. Hope was back, even though I knew her long, tough road was likely to get even tougher.

THINGS TO CONSIDER

Whether you see the day as dark and hopeless or bright and promising depends largely on your personal viewpoint. Your perception really can make a cloudy day seem sunny, and the opposite is equally true.

A useful analogy is the camera. Think about the various lenses that a photographer uses. If it's a dark day and he wants his photos to look sunnier, he might choose a yellow tinted lens; to warm up a picture, a red lens; to make a winter scene feel even colder, a blue lens.

You, too, use a lens to view the events of your day, and it changes your outlook much like the tinted camera lens changes a photo. Sometime you may view a problem in a humorous vein and see the funny side of everything. Or you use a negative lens that makes the tiniest problem appear unsolvable. A positive lens allows you to find a thread of hope even in failure. Potential insults and accusations often fail to register because you're focused on the good news, instead of straining to hear the bad.

To correct depression, it is critical that you learn to choose the correct lenses. Your choice can make the difference between hope and despair (yours *and* others').

TRY THIS . . .

During the next few days, see if you can recognize yourself using the wrong lens to see certain events that impact your life. If so, make a list of these situations in your journal and indicate whether you were able to improve your outlook by deliberately switching to a more positive viewpoint. If you were able to switch to a more positive perspective, note and remember how you did this.

69
SOLUTION

BALANCE YOUR LIFE

*A*nita and I are on our way back from Vermont today. She's driving and I'm relaxing here in the passenger seat, writing notes in my journal. This is my ninth or tenth page, and words flow so freely that I have trouble writing fast enough to capture them on the paper. My thoughts are of optimism and promise, leaving doubt far behind. It feels like someone has opened a window wide to the world and beckoned me to come and see the goodness that I've been missing. The sun dances across the hillsides of my mind and the proverbial bluebird chirps songs of joy and happiness. I feel surrounded by the harmony that's been missing lately from my life.

How can such exuberance be possible, I wonder? Four short days ago I faced a wall of despair so despicable that I could hardly find even a trace of hope in my surroundings. Now everything seems changed.

When the idea for this mini-vacation initially surfaced, my first thought was, "Impossible! I don't have time for any trip. I'm too busy. I have obligations—things that have to get done." *My mood problems have made it difficult for me to keep up lately. Finally, when I began to realize that I was accomplishing very little anyway, I agreed to go. "What does it matter?" I lamented.*

Little did I know that these few days would provide fresh perspectives and new insights that would distance me from my depression. Stepping back from my old obligations has cleared my mind and corrected my compass. Letting go has opened my mind to new avenues of possibility. My heart is once again ready for the challenges that lie ahead.

THINGS TO CONSIDER

A wheel that's out of balance wobbles and shakes until it finally flies apart, and this same principle applies to your life. To stay on an even keel, you need to find ways to balance the various activities you're involved in. We've all heard the old saying, "All work and no play makes Johnny a dull boy," but the damage goes even beyond dullness. Allowing time for many different activities helps you see the big picture and maintain accurate perspectives for your life. Exercise, work, friends, hobbies, vacations, etc., help provide the variety needed to recharge your mind with clear thinking. Determination is important, but knocking your head against a wall too long damages your chances of success. Time away from a project or problem is often a more effective way to infuse your mind with better ideas and new solutions.

We all know that a balanced diet is an important factor for maintaining a healthy body, and balancing your life with a variety of worthwhile activities helps achieve a healthy mind. It's one more tool to help you drive depression from your life.

Try This . . .

Make a note about some project or problem that you have become so wrapped up in that you're having trouble seeing clearly. Then resolve to step back from the pressure for a while and focus on other things that allow your mind to clear. When you return to the problem, observe whether this time away was beneficial in providing new insights for resolving your difficulty. If you learn to use this simple tactic, the rewards are clearer thinking and balanced living.

PRACTICE PATIENCE

— From My Journal —

Yesterday my grandson and I planted marigold seeds in a Styrofoam cup. When we finished, he handled the watering and I helped him find a place for the cup on the kitchen windowsill. Not more than an hour later, I found him standing there waiting for the seeds to sprout. I chuckled to myself as I tried to explain the concept of time and the need to be patient to a three-year-old. His lack of understanding reminded me of my own impatience, which has complicated my recovery from depression. My hopes have been dashed enough times by depression that I should have learned by now to focus on the long view.

Surprisingly, depression provides many euphoric occasions, often without a hint of warning, when my dark moods lift like a cloud to reveal the sun again. Some of these reprieves stretch out for weeks, even months, and I begin to think my ordeal might be over for good. But each time my dreary mood returns to engulf me again in those same feelings of melancholy. My lack of patience too often convinces me that I'm being pushed back to the recovery starting line. But the truth is that each episode is part of the healing process.

Searching for a better way to cope with these ups and downs, I now use a strategy I call "Work & Wait." It teaches me that almost nothing about this mood illness is permanent, regardless of whether I find myself in a state of torment or basking in the joy of euphoria. It helps me to view the events of each day more objectively and find the thread of hope that sustains my optimism. So I have learned to wait—wait as patiently as I can—for the day when those dark clouds are gone for good and sunshine spills back into my life to stay.

THINGS TO CONSIDER

If depression teaches you nothing else worthwhile, it's almost sure to teach you patience. When you start antidepressant medications, it often takes several weeks to determine the correct dosage and to judge the effectiveness. Positive results from other therapies also take time, and the waiting can be difficult to endure. When you're feeling good, you want to believe that your low moods are gone forever. But when your feelings swing to the morose side, you often can't detect even a trace of hope in depression's dark tunnel. During those days, depression feels equally permanent. Life feels like it's out of control as your moods race up and down without reason or warning.

Depression can play this game with you only so many times before you begin to catch on. You realize that you need to temper your reaction, regardless of the direction that your mood is swinging, by taking a *wait and see* approach. Think of patience as the ballast that evens out the highs and lows and helps you maintain balance. It makes you less inclined to give up on your therapy or to give in to a lifetime of depression. Developing greater patience not only improves your prognosis, it offers you a lifelong gift of greater serenity.

TRY THIS . . .

> Think about recent events that relate to your depression illness, and try to remember a recent occasion when your lack of patience caused you unnecessary anxiety. Write an abbreviated account of this problem in your journal and explain how a more patient approach might have eased your distress. Learn to use patience to level out your life.

71
SOLUTION

YOU ARE NOT ALONE

— From My Journal —

What a shock! I went to the Fairmont Hotel across from the airport tonight to listen to a woman speak about anxiety and depression. I'd seen the notice in the newspaper, but I was hesitant to attend. (I hate to get hassled.) After vacillating all day about whether to go, I finally dredged up enough courage to put on a clean shirt and take off before I could change my mind again. I got to the hotel early, so I circled the block to chew up some time. Then a couple of minutes before the seminar was to start, I parked my car and headed for the door. My plan was to find an inconspicuous seat near the back where I could listen without becoming involved in any way.

The surprise came when I pulled open the door of the banquet hall and found the room jammed with hundreds of people. At first I panicked, but then I saw an empty chair in the far corner. Trying to act nonchalant about the whole thing, I worked my way over to it and slid into the seat. The seminar was late starting, and most of the people around me were engaged in conversation. In fact there was so much talking, smiling, and gesturing that I began to wonder if I might be in the wrong room. I had expected a seminar on depression to attract a much smaller, more somber group.

I had trouble hearing the speaker from my seat in the back of the auditorium, but it really didn't matter. My feelings of isolation and apprehension were quickly draining away, replaced by a sense of belonging. I wasn't alone in my battle with depression.

If someone had unknowingly wandered into that banquet hall tonight, that person could never have guessed the bond that brought us all together.

Things to Consider

Many valuable resources are available to help solve your depression. Yet most of these won't be offered unless you have the courage to ask for help. Reaching out may sound easy, but fear often taunts you with warnings that people will think you're weak, incapable, or even a little crazy. Should you take the chance of ridicule to find the help you need, or play it safe and remain on the pathway of gloom and grief? This can be a wrenching dilemma for those who suffer from mood disorders.

Depression teaches many lessons, and one of them is that learning to reach out for help will make you stronger, *not* weaker. In fact learning to team up with others can be the beginning of a new way of thinking that makes life more inclusive and satisfying. Interdependency can become the bond that frees you from isolation and lets you begin healing. Sometimes your role will be that of the recipient of care; at other times you become the caregiver. "Together" is a frame of mind that can open up your world.

TRY THIS . . .

Make a list of three places or events that you would consider reaching out to for help in solving your depression. Select the one that seems like the best place to start, push aside any fears, and give it a try. Your effort may move you closer to recovery.

PREPARE FOR CHANGE

— From My Journal —

Another note from Anita

Dear Dick,

I hope you won't mind me adding this little note to your journal, because there's something I want you to know. It's about me, and how lucky I feel to be with you. It's about us, and the way this struggle with depression has welded us together. It's about living and the lessons we've learned that make life more precious, more wonderful, than I ever thought possible. Clearly you're not the person you were when this bewildering depression began, but neither am I. I can't help but marvel how so many blessings can come from such a contemptible illness. Life does provide some interesting perplexities, doesn't it? Is it any wonder we confuse good and bad?

All this depression stuff I'll never understand, and I won't lie and say it's been easy on any of us. But what is clear to me is the abundant joy that life has left us in the wake of a nightmare that I

sometimes thought would never end. No, you are not the man I
married; you are more . . . so much more.

You are my rock,
Love,
Anita

THINGS TO CONSIDER

Even as an adult I love kaleidoscopes, with their sparkle of ever-changing shapes and colors, but it's the first kaleidoscope I received as a small child that holds the most treasured spot in my heart. I thought it like magic how the picture would completely change with every tiny twist.

People change much the same way as the kaleidoscope, and the turbulence of depression provides the opportunity for you to reinvent a sparkling new life. As much as you may yearn to get back to the old *you* that existed before this devastating illness began, you eventually realize that's not possible. You can't go back to yesterday, no matter how longingly you wish for your old life. But the good news is that you have the power to influence life's changes and move in the direction of your choice. Change offers you a second chance to ground yourself in more solid values, to see your world from a clearer perspective, and to accept life—warts and all.

Unguided change can make you bitter and cranky if you allow yourself to wallow in the trenches of negativity, bemoan how unfair life has been, and dwell on the rotten deal that depression dealt you. It is your choice, so grab the wheel and choose your course, to become the architect of change in your life. The reward is happiness beyond all your expectations.

Try This . . .

Become the architect of the new life you choose to live. Using the lessons of your experience with depression, design a better life that's filled with serenity, purpose, and the things that you want and need. Begin now to put it on paper and prepare those plans. Start building a life that fulfills your hopes of tomorrow.

TORMENT TO TRIUMPH

— From My Journal —

It was one of those perfect fall days today, with golden leaves raining down from the tall maple trees in the yard. I love to shuffle through those deep, dry leaves and fill my head with the rich aroma of autumn. It's so good just to be alive today and feeling great again.

Gone are those despicable voices of depression that haunted me for so long, replaced now by a growing sense of happiness. The priorities of my life have been rearranged with new insights that put me in tune with the world, instead of leaving me mired in the menacing self-doubt of the past.

This new perspective didn't come cheaply but, since I was given no option, I refuse to dwell on the staggering price I've paid. I won't soon forget the years of bewilderment I spent being ambushed by new aspects of depression. It happened on a daily basis, it seemed.

Thank God that somewhere in my being was a tenacity that wouldn't let me surrender. I can't begin to count the battles I've lost, but still I hung on and hung on and hung on. I was determined to reclaim my life, no matter how tough the fight or how long it might take.

On days like today, it feels so good to be back in control of my mind. Still, I feel no arrogance in victory. Instead I strive to remain strong and vigilant. Who can say when the black dog of depression might again be waiting outside my door? I'm determined to be armed and ready just in case it ever tries to return.

THINGS TO CONSIDER

The intent of most of us, at the beginning anyway, is to somehow get back to the person we were before depression first nailed us. This is a laudable goal, but in truth it's a goal that's often impossible. The ordeal of your illness has changed you in ways that previously you could not have imagined. Both physically and mentally you've been severely tested, but you have endured.

Finally, you can sense sustained improvement; your long bout with depression is lifting. You're anxious to return to the life you used to know. But slowly the realization sinks in that you can never be the person you were when this trial began. You have been transformed, transformed like a soldier who has experienced the nightmare of battle and now sees the world in a different light. You can choose to rail about how unfair life has been to you, or you can apply the lessons of depression to find a greater joy and appreciation for living than you have ever known. It's your opportunity to turn torment into triumph.

Divide a sheet of paper in half vertically. On the left side, list some of the characteristics of the "old you" that may have contributed to your problems with depression. Then on the right side, list the characteristics that are part of the "new you." This sounder approach to life becomes your evidence of having rounded the corner that leads back to normalcy.

SEEK ENCHANTMENT

— FROM MY JOURNAL —

"I *don't feel like it," are the words that seem most often to come from my mouth when I can't quickly think of the other ninety-nine reasons why I don't want to do something. But even though I don't like cooking myself in the sun, I agreed to go on this seaside vacation with Anita. We've been here almost a week now. I can't recall when I have ever felt so in touch with the world, and so far away from depression.*

I've been getting up early, while Anita is still asleep, and walking the beaches just as the sun begins to edge over the far horizon. It's an indescribable feeling to look out to an azure sky as the waves race over my bare feet and stretch out to kiss the sand beyond. I have a profound understanding that everything I see, from the sand and sky and boulders to the islands beyond, has been here for a million years before I got here, and will be here for millions more after I leave. The agony of my illness seems like it took place eons ago. I feel connected now to the universe, where peace, beauty, and order prevail.

This morning I've brought my journal along on my beach walk to record my thoughts of this place. Yet I've sat here on a stone ledge overlooking the ocean for more than an hour without finishing the entry. I write words, then cross them out because they seem so tame compared to the immense feelings that flood my soul. My prayer is that God will paint this place so vividly in my mind that it can never fade away.

THINGS TO CONSIDER

Close your eyes and ask yourself this question: *"Where, in all the world, is the most enchanting place I've ever been?"* Was it the veranda of your childhood home? Summer camp? A Caribbean island where you vacationed? Maybe your grandparents' rustic cabin, tucked away in the deep woods? Or a honeymoon cottage on Nantucket? It makes no difference if it's around the corner from your present home, or an ocean (or half-century) away. What's important is that your memory of the place be so unforgettable that you can instantly flash it onto the screen of your mind and be mentally carried back there again and again. Perhaps you can still hear the voices of long ago or the sound of waves crashing against the boulders. Can you picture the evening sunset radiating across the bay or find the moon still locked in place between the cypress trees as it was on the night you left?

Such imaginary trips may last for only a few rapturous moments, but this can be long enough to catch your breath and restore a positive outlook. This is not a flight from reality but a "time out" that you can use to check your compass and confirm your direction before continuing the day's journey.

TRY THIS . . .

Begin this exercise by finding a quiet place that shuts out the din around you. Then close your eyes and search your memory for those special occasions in your past that were enchantingly joyful. Try to remember the smells, and sounds, and voices. Recall the people and circumstances that made these times so remarkable for you. Then single out one place—the one that stirs the most poignant memories in your soul—and try to record it forever in your memory. The ability to transport your mind back to this special place can become the bridge that carries you across life's troubling times.

75
SOLUTION

SHOUT FOR JOY

— From My Journal —

I sift through my feelings tonight as I contemplate what I will write in my journal. It's been several months since my last entry and I thumb back through the pages, reading an excerpt here and there. Suddenly, I realize how much everything has changed. My mind, which had been languid for so long, is now stirring with new challenges. Joy and expectancy have replaced my apathy.

For many months, I've sensed that depression has been slowly losing its grip on me, but exactly when it finally disappeared, I can't say. Reading my old journal entries now makes me realize that I'm no longer the victim who wrote those agonizing lines. My grounded boat has broken free and is again skimming along with full sails and great promise.

It's funny, but I'm almost afraid to keep reading, afraid that my writings from those dark and troubling days of the past still have the power to pull me back, afraid the phantom voices that traumatized me with wretched lies for so long might start up again. In defiance,

I keep turning the pages. My fear turns to exhilaration as I discover that those terrible thoughts can no longer torment me. I am free!

Still, this illness has taught me not to gloat over victory. Instead I make myself a promise that I will keep working to strengthen my mind, that I will keep learning to appreciate life, living moment by moment instead of betting everything on the future. For now, though, I rejoice that the victory I have worked and waited for so long is finally here. It makes me want to shout with joy!

THINGS TO CONSIDER

Even as you struggle to overcome this agonizing illness you're probably wondering how your depression will finally end. Perhaps you're hoping to wake up some morning to discover that a miracle has taken place. Yesterday's deep melancholy has vanished—gone forever—and you're back to your old self again.

Not likely.

A more common scenario is that after what seemed like an eternity of ups and downs, you realize one day that depression no longer holds the top spot among your problems. You may still have gray days when your outlook tilts toward the negative, but they are much less frequent now. And, although depression still harasses you occasionally, it doesn't devastate you like before.

The demise of depression is like a long winter that delivers spring after many false starts and broken promises. Depression's power over you slowly diminishes until it finally disappears almost unnoticed. As this happens, your clear thinking gradually returns and you become fully immersed in life again. Realistic expectations and accurate perspectives become the framework of your everyday thinking. You are more than a survivor; *you* are a winner.

Try This . . .

Depression is an illness that requires a lifetime of vigilance. Your vulnerability makes it important for you to review and adjust your attitudes and perspectives often. Take a few minutes and think about various aspects of your life that may need additional effort. Then record these ideas in your journal and decide how best to implement them.

A NOTE
FROM THE AUTHOR'S WIFE

Finally—it's over. Dick has been depression-free for several years now. I begin this note with that wonderful news because that's the only *good* part of this dreadful ordeal. At first I was naive enough to think it was *Dick's* depression, but I soon found the struggle affected everyone in our family. There seemed to be so little I could do to help except plead with God—asking Him to return Dick to the exuberant person he used to be, and to restore us to the happy, carefree family we had been before this illness began.

Early on, Dick chose to hide his depression, knowing the stigma and concerned about ridicule. Although I might have chosen a different course, I honored his secret. When other people asked sensitive questions, I covered for him. I pretended that the children and I were doing fine—that his depression didn't affect us much. Even when there was nothing but bleakness and despair I smiled, put up a good front, and pretended that everything was just fine. Outwardly I hid my feelings of desperation, but inside I craved even a glimmer of sunlight for our family. I hated the very word *depression* and everything it implied. It was like a pall had been draped over us and we could find no way to pull it back. So we hung on—not because we were strong, but because we seemed to have no other choice. We hoped and prayed and cried, but we refused to give up.

The big breakthrough we begged for never came. Instead, splinters of hope began appearing, almost imperceptibly at first, to penetrate our darkness. Dick began to visit with old friends again, play with the children, or putter in his workshop. I'll never forget the afternoon I first heard him roar with his old laughter. It surprised me so much that I rushed to the back porch and found him standing at the window watching the kids out in the yard trying to catch our new puppy. Instantly I threw my arms around him, unable to stop the tears of relief sliding down my face. Not a word was said about breakthroughs that day, yet we both knew another wall of depression had crumbled. The constant fatigue that had plagued Dick for so long was better now, so we could go shopping or take the kids to a movie on occasion. But even as joy returned, our skepticism lingered on. We had been chased up and down the mountainsides of depression for so long that we felt like we could only whisper about this new hope now filling our lives.

In truth, Dick never returned to his old self, and my prayer of having our family return to the life we had known before this trial began was not to be, either. We couldn't go back; the pain and suffering had changed us too much. Before this ordeal began, Dick and I had been primarily focused on the future. Our quest for pride and perfection was immense and *things* were very important to us. But depression changed all that. Our Pollyanna theories about the perfect home, the perfect family, the perfect everything, were gone. Gone, too, was much of our arrogance, impatience, and insensitivity with others. People are now so much more important to us than things, and each new day is a gift that we can't wait to unwrap and enjoy.

Anita

A FINAL WORD

I have no idea how many spiral notebooks I've filled since my war with depression began. My journalizing habit continues long after the most recent battles with this illness subsided. It's been a harrowing journey, one that's ripped open my life and forced me to find my *real* self among the ruins. Many "whys" remain, but I have little desire to waste time pursuing them.

One of the most astounding discoveries from this experience was learning that depression wears so many deceptive faces. Early on, I felt certain that I could recognize the symptoms of my suffering. Now, years later, armed with greater knowledge and the gift of experience, I find that many people who suffer from depression display few recognizable clues to their ailment. Recently, an upbeat friend whom I have known for more than twenty years revealed to me her own "battle of the blues." Not in a million years would I have guessed. There are countless people who grapple with this torment and still manage to go to work every day. Others have difficulty finding the strength to get out of bed each morning. I have found no norm, no template that puts an accurate face on this illness.

Depression seems to have a long menu of burdens which it indiscriminately doles out to its victims in various forms and amounts. Still, for everyone involved, it's a scary detour with few road signs, mileposts, or directions. All you can do is try to hold the wheel steady as you search for a way back to the mainstream of life.

Reference books sometimes refer to *serious* depression, but those who suffer it know that there is no other kind. The consensus among medical experts seems to be that this disorder results from a chemical imbalance in the brain, but the question remains: Does depression cause this imbalance, does the imbalance cause the depression, or does it involve a bit of both? I certainly don't know the answer to that question, but I'm thankful that thousands of dedicated researchers are working every day to defeat all forms of depressive illnesses.

All of us, regardless of how we are connected to this affliction, have a responsibility to do whatever we can to bring light and understanding to those caught in an ordeal that has been misunderstood for too long. Depression is a *real* illness that can be successfully treated. This simple fact needs to be understood by everyone, because none of us knows whose doorway may be draped in melancholy tomorrow.

FAMOUS PEOPLE
WITH DEPRESSION

This list of famous persons known to have experienced one or more types of depression is long and, remarkably, only a sampling. The intent is not to glorify depression in any way but to illustrate the pervasiveness of the problem and assure you that you have not been singled out to suffer alone. This list includes people who made significant accomplishments in spite of their depression.

Edwin "Buzz" Aldrin
Ludwig van Beethoven
John Berryman
Art Buchwald
Truman Capote
Winston Churchill
Tyrus Cobb
Rodney Dangerfield
Emily Dickinson
James Farmer

Honoré de Balzac
Irving Berlin
Terry Bradshaw
Barbara Bush
Ray Charles
Rosemary Clooney
Calvin Coolidge
John Denver
Ralph Waldo Emerson
William Faulkner

F. Scott Fitzgerald

Judy Garland

Graham Green

Ernest Hemingway

Howard Hughes

William James

Danny Kaye

Abraham Lincoln

Michelangelo

Marilyn Monroe

Deborah Norville

Boris Pasternak

Jane Pauley

Sylvia Plath

Cole Porter

Yves Saint Laurent

William Sherman

Diana Spencer

William Styron

Dylan Thomas

Leo Tolstoy

Vincent Van Gogh

Walt Whitman

Jonathan Winters

Tammy Wynette

Boris Yeltsin

John Kenneth Galbraith

Tipper Gore

George Frideric Handel

Audrey Hepburn

Edward Hopper

Ashley Judd

Vivien Leigh

Herman Melville

Claude Monet

Richard Nixon

Eugene O'Neill

George Patton

J.C. Penney

Edgar Allan Poe

John Ruskin

Anne Sexton

Paul Simon

Robert Lewis Stevenson

Peter Tchaikovsky

Gene Tierney

Spencer Tracy

Mike Wallace

Tennessee Williams

Virginia Woolf

Bert Yancy

RECOMMENDED READING

The books listed below are those that were useful to me during my own struggle with depression. However, each of us has different needs, so make your own search to find the books that are most helpful to you.

Bloch, Douglas. *When Going Through Hell . . . Don't Stop: A Survivor's Guide to Overcoming Anxiety and Clinical Depression.* Portland, OR: Pallas Communications, 1999.

Burns, David D. *Feeling Good: The New Mood Therapy.* New York, NY: HarperCollins, 2000. Originally published in 1980.

Dyer, Wayne W. *You'll See It When You Believe It: The Way to Your Personal Transformation.* New York, NY: William Morrow, 1989.

Luciani, Joseph J. *Self Coaching: How to Heal Anxiety and Depression.* San Francisco, CA: Jossey-Bass (an imprint of Wiley), 2002.

Mundy, Linus. *Elf-Help for Overcoming Depression: How to Look into One's Own Heart and Soul, and to Others for Help.* (Elf Self Help Series.) St. Meinrad, IN: Abbey Press, 1998.

Seligman, Martin E. *Learned Optimism: How to Change Your Mind and Your Life.* NY: Simon and Schuster, 1990 and 1998.

Simon, Julian L. *Good Mood: The New Psychology of Overcoming Depression.* Peru, IL: Open Court Publishing (Carus), 1993.

Thompson, Tracy. *The Beast: A Journey Through Depression.* New York, NY: Plume Edition, 1996.

Yapko, Michael D. *Breaking the Patterns of Depression.* New York, NY: Doubleday, 1997.

ORGANIZATIONS AND WEB SITES WITH RESOURCES FOR DEPRESSION, ANXIETY, AND MOOD DISORDERS

The web has become such a valuable source of information that it's a great place to begin your search for information and resources. Listed below are a few of the many excellent web sites available.

AMERICAN PSYCHIATRIC ASSOCIATION
Web site: *www.psych.org*
1000 Wilson Boulevard, Suite 1825
Arlington, VA 22209-3901
Phone 703–907–7300

AMERICAN PSYCHOLOGICAL ASSOCIATION
Web site: *www.apa.org*
750 First Street, NE
Washington, DC 20002–4242
Phone 800–374–2721

ANXIETY DISORDERS ASSOCIATION OF AMERICA
Web site: *www.adaa.org*
8730 Georgia Avenue, Suite 600
Silver Spring, MD 20910
Phone 240–485–1001

DEPRESSION AND BIPOLAR SUPPORT ALLIANCE
Web site: *www.dbsalliance.org*
730 N. Franklin Street, Suite 501
Chicago, IL 60610–7224
Phone 800–826–3632

DEPRESSION.COM
Web site: *www.depression.com*
Understanding and treating depression
Funded and developed by GlaxoSmithKline

DR. IVAN'S DEPRESSION CENTRAL
Web site: *www.psycom.net/depression.central.html*
This site is a clearing house for information on all types of
depressive orders and the most effective treatments; main-
tained independently by Dr. Ivan Goldberg, psychiatrist and
clinical psychopharmacologist in private practice in New
York City

McMAN'S DEPRESSION AND BIPOLAR WEB
Web site: *www.mcmanweb.com*
Created by John McManamy, who has himself struggled with
bipolar disorder
Information, chat, personal stories, links

NATIONAL ALLIANCE FOR THE MENTALLY ILL (NAMI)
Web site: *www.nami.org*
Colonial Place Three
2107 Wilson Boulevard, Suite 300
Arlington, VA 22201–3042
Phone: 800–950–NAMI (6264)

NATIONAL FOUNDATION FOR DEPRESSIVE ILLNESS
Web site: *www.depression.org*
P.O. Box 2257
New York, NY 10116
Phone: 800–239–1265

NATIONAL INSTITUTE OF MENTAL HEALTH
Web site: *www.nimh.nih.gov*
6001 Executive Boulevard, Room 8184, MSC 9663
Bethesda, MD 20892–9663
Phone: 866–615–6464 (toll free)

NATIONAL MENTAL HEALTH ASSOCIATION
Web site: *www.nmha.org*
2001 N. Beauregard Street, 12th Floor
Alexandria, VA 22311
Phone: 800–969–NMHA (6642)

NATIONAL MENTAL HEALTH INFORMATION CENTER
Web site: *www.mentalhealth.samhsa.gov*
P.O Box 42557
Washington, DC 20015
Phone: 800–789–2647

ACKNOWLEDGMENTS

I never could claim to be a particularly religious person, although I'm definitely a believer. That's why it's shocking to admit that I may really be God's ghostwriter for this book.

When the thought first entered my head—to write a book about depression based on my personal experiences with this illness—I dismissed it without a moment's consideration. I had seen enough of depression; all I wanted to do was to forget it and move on. Besides, I wasn't the right person to write such a book, I told myself, even though I had overcome this dreaded disorder. Each time the thought of writing such a book resurfaced, I rejected it and reminded myself that I already had several unfinished writing projects waiting to be completed.

In spite of my constant rejection of the idea of a book about depression, I soon found myself at the computer, pounding out stories about my torment and the path I followed to recovery. I found myself unable to concentrate on my other writing projects, truly compelled to write this book instead. By now I was searching through old depression journals I had written long before and digging deep in my memory to understand and relate both the melancholy and the triumph of my ordeal. Mentally reliving these terrible times often felt so real that I feared being drawn back into depression's shadow again. On several occasions I put my depression-book stuff away and told my wife I couldn't do it. I was giving up on the idea for good. Every time, though, before many days had passed, I would find myself working on the book again.

I continued this *on again, off again* depression book effort until one spring day when nothing seemed to be going right with the book. My computer had lost a number of files that I had spent days revising. I became angry and tossed the complete notebook in the trash, printouts and all, and started out the door of my small studio in the woods. I was through, *definitely* finished working on this depression book.

I hesitated in the doorway, looking up at the overcast sky, sad because I was scrapping a project I had wasted so much time on, but looking forward to getting back to my other writing. That's when the *real* Author of this book made His claim in a single beam of sunlight that broke through the darkened sky and shone directly on my face. It was almost like a blinding spotlight directed right at me. I can still feel the uplifting warmth that radiated through my whole body in those few short moments and the unmistakable but silent voice that registered in my mind. I can't recall the message, word for word, but even in my dazed state I was certain: The voice belonged to God. Clearly He was telling me He wanted the depression book completed and was offering His help. It was in that moment that I first realized that this was really God's book, and I was His ghostwriter. In truth, I'm a rather pragmatic person who has never placed much credibility in such religious epiphanies, but on that day I had no doubt that I'd felt a direct connection to my Maker.

That divine experience sent me back to work on the book with a new passion, and from that time forward the support quickly surfaced to make this book a reality. First I found Ed Stackler on the Web. He's a book editor I had come to know fifteen years earlier but had lost track of when he moved from New York to California. I think of him as the angel God sent to provide assistance and encouragement. Without him, this book would never have happened. Then Faith Hamlin came on the scene as my very astute and effective agent. I remember writing on the cover of my journal that day *"have faith"* and that's what I got. And finally Matthew Lore of Marlowe & Company/Avalon Publishing read my manuscript and immediately called with an offer to publish it. I knew, even back then, that little of this was of my own doing. Somewhere out there is a power much larger than myself who brings this book to you. Call it whatever you prefer, but I see myself as a ghostwriter for God.

PLEASE WRITE

I would love to hear from you if you feel this book has benefited you or someone you care about. Which stories or advice were most helpful, and how did you apply the suggestions in this book to your situation? Especially welcome are your own journal writings, stories, poetry and other ideas that have helped you overcome the agony of depression. My hope is that by sharing some of your inspiring words in a follow-up book or on my Web site www.moodlifters.com, we may offer help and comfort to others who battle this illness. Your material may be either typewritten or in longhand, and it does not have to be in a publishable form. You can email it to me at dick@moodlifters.com or send it by the U.S. Postal Service. If you prefer that your name not be used, please write DO NOT SHARE MY NAME boldly at the top of each page. Unless you write otherwise, by sending me your thoughts and experiences you'll be granting me permission to publish your material. You have my assurance that no names or addresses will be shared without your specific permission.

If the material you are sharing is not your own, please include the source and name of the author, if known. I look forward to hearing from you.

Richard Rybolt
3593 Medina Road
Medina, OH 44256
dick@moodlifters.com